LIFESAVING

RESCUE and WATER SAFETY

LIFESAVING

RESCUE and WATER SAFETY

Prepared by
The American National Red Cross
With 240 Illustrations

Fourth Printing 1977

DOUBLEDAY & COMPANY, INC.
GARDEN CITY, N.Y.

Library of Congress Cataloging in Publication Data

Red Cross. United States. American National Red Cross.
  Lifesaving; rescue and water safety

  1. Life-saving. 2. Swimming. 3. Aquatic sports—Safety
measures. I. Mongeon, Edmond J. II. Title. 3. Respiration,
[DNLM: 1. Accident prevention. 2. First aid. 3. Respiration,
Artificial. W0700 R312UL fl GV 837.R4 1974 614.8'1
74-13256 ISBN 0-385-06349-0

Library of Congress Catalog Card No. 74-13256
Printed in the United States of America

PREFACE

Safety in and on the water depends upon a number of things. It begins, of course, with the ability to swim well enough to care for one's self under ordinary conditions. It does not, however, end there. Real water safety is also based upon such factors as the ability to recognize and avoid hazardous water conditions and practices. Ability to use self-rescue skills to get out of dangerous situations is also a factor. Finally, skill in rescuing or assisting persons in danger of drowning is a means of preserving a person's own life as well as saving that of someone else. The three major causes of drowning are, and always have been, failure to recognize hazardous conditions or practices, inability to get out of dangerous situations, and lack of knowledge of safe ways in which to aid persons requiring assistance in the water.

When Commodore Wilbert E. Longfellow started the Life Saving Service of the American Red Cross in 1914, he concentrated wisely on the organization and training of volunteer lifesaving corps throughout the country to supervise otherwise unguarded bathing beaches. It soon became evident, however, that this was not the final solution to the problem of drownings, and changes in methods were reflected in the slogan coined by the Commodore: "Everyone a swimmer, every swimmer a lifesaver." The slogan reflects the philosophy that the best kind of lifesaving is being able to swim well, and that the next best way to cope with the accidental drowning situation is to train as many people as possible in lifesaving techniques.

Since 1914, the American Red Cross has published various texts, planned and written as resources to which anyone interested in water safety may refer. The books have been designed as texts upon which Red Cross lifesaving training courses are based and have been used by both instructors and pupils as authoritative sources of information.

The present text, developed by Edmond J. Mongeon, national director of the American Red Cross Water Safety Program, is the resource textbook for Red Cross lifesaving and water safety courses and is dedicated to the task of teaching and disseminating the skills of lifesaving and water safety.

ACKNOWLEDGMENTS

The American Red Cross wishes to acknowledge with appreciation the contributions made by Carroll L. Bryant and Richard L. Brown, former directors of its Water Safety Program. Much of the material is based on the 1938 textbook *Life Saving and Water Safety,* which was written by Mr. Bryant, and on the information contained in a number of instructor manuals later written by Mr. Brown.

Special acknowledgment and thanks are extended to the following lifesaving advisory committee, which met several times and gave a great deal of guidance, advice, and direction to the text contents: Mrs. Prudence Fleming, formerly of Temple University and past chairman, Council for National Cooperation in Aquatics (CNCA); Mrs. Ruth Magher, Spartanburg, S.C., formerly affiliated with Queens College; Dr. Robert Bartels, Ohio State University; Charles C. Stott, North Carolina State University; Ralph Flanagan, Los Angeles Chapter, American Red Cross; and John T. Goetz, Southeastern Pennsylvania Chapter, American Red Cross.

The revision of the lifesaving information was initiated at the Red Cross Lifesaving and Water Safety Symposium held in Washington, D.C., in 1969. At that time, in addition to the above committee, some 25 aquatics leaders representing 20 national agencies and organizations explored all the major aspects of water safety for the Red Cross to consider in bringing its material up to date.

In addition, the writer has drawn heavily upon the experience of hundreds of professional and volunteer water safety staff in the field, and at American Red Cross national headquarters, and of other water safety specialists as well. The advice and the cooperation of all these individuals are greatly appreciated.

CONTENTS

LIFESAVING

RESCUE and WATER SAFETY

1

PERSONAL SAFETY
IN THE AQUATIC ENVIRONMENT

Human beings do not naturally belong in the water. Their whole physical makeup—posture, body temperature, breathing apparatus, shape and arrangement of arms and legs, specific gravity, functions, everything—have been developed for terrestrial living. There is literally nothing to indicate anything natural about man's aquatic activities, yet an unbounded curiosity, a dominant will, and a marvelously adaptable brain and physical structure have not only urged humans into the water but have also prompted them to develop forms of locomotion suited to their needs in the new element. Individuals have found comfort, relaxation, and enjoyment in the water. At the same time, however, experience has taught them that in the water there are definite limits beyond which they cannot safely go, and there is a certain amount of knowledge of the aquatic environment that they must acquire. Humans are one of the few animals—if not the only animal—that must learn how to swim.

Drowning is simply suffocation in the water. When the water closes over the mouth and nose and people are in such a position or condition that they cannot surface to breathe, drowning occurs. Learning how to swim, knowing when and where to swim, and being prepared for the hazards of the aquatic environment will equip a person with the major defenses against drowning and will enhance enjoyment of the aquatic environment.

In personal safety the first rule is to learn to swim and to swim well. The American Red Cross, as well as many other agencies, schools, camps, recreation programs, and individuals, provides swimming instruction. The time devoted to swimming instruction is well spent indeed.

WHEN TO SWIM

There is little question concerning the time of year to swim out of doors. Temperature and weather conditions dictate the swimming season to all but the exceptional swimmer. In some southern latitudes the swimming season extends over the entire year, while in some northern areas it may be but a few weeks. With the increased popularity of indoor facilities, covered pools, and heated water, the length of the swimming season has increased. When the water ranges in temperature from 70 to 78 degrees it is, apparently, most inviting to man.

The time of day when a person should swim is not particularly important as long as the applicable safety rules are observed, such as not swimming immediately after eating, when overheated, or during an electrical storm. Overexposure to sun rays should be avoided, particularly during midday. Chilling should be avoided on cool, overcast days.

The "morning dip," a quick plunge taken immediately upon rising, can provide real pleasure and exhilaration to the individual who can stand the shock of cool air and cool water and who reacts well to the experience. Some persons are rugged enough physically to enjoy a morning dip and benefit by it without any special preparation. Others can accustom themselves to it gradually by warming up easily before entering the water and by beginning with only the briefest periods of immersion. However, there are many to whom the quick transition from a warm bed to the chilled morning air and water is not only distasteful but also quite lacking in benefit, and sometimes actually injurious to health. Briefly, it may be said that the "morning dip" should be made a matter of individual choice.

The "starlight dip," or night swim, is a thrilling experience, and no one who has ever enjoyed a cooling dip just before retiring on a still, hot night can easily forget its pleasant qualities. When a person swims well, thoroughly knows the swimming place, stays close to shallow water, is accompanied by other swimmers, and follows good safety practices, there is little danger in a starlight dip.

The length of time a person may stay in the water without ill effect is governed by the sense of physical comfort. Usually, when people become chilled, enervated, or tired they begin to feel uncomfortable and get out of the water of their own volition. However, children frequently allow their sense of enjoyment to outweigh a growing feeling of discomfort and unduly prolong their periods of immersion. Uncontrollable shivering, a bluish tinge to the lips, a drawn or pinched face, and cold and clammy skin are indications that it is time to come out.

A large percentage of drownings occur early in the swimming season when individuals (usually young boys) decide to take the first few swims of the year. They are naturally out of condition for swimming and overestimate their ability and endurance in attempting to do what they were capable of doing when the season closed the previous year. The onset of "early season" fatigue may be very rapid, and the individual who has unwisely swum away from shore into deep water may be in grave danger.

WHERE TO SWIM

Many types of swimming areas exist, from the old swimming hole to the modern natatorium. Obviously, one of the first principles of water safety is to choose a safe place in which to swim. Common sense should guide a person to select a site designed for swimming and one that provides the protection of lifeguards. In the absence of such sites, a person should consider the many factors of a safe swimming area before selecting a place to swim. Unsupervised swimming in rivers, ponds, quarries, and lakes and at ocean beaches exposes a person to certain hazards that can prove dangerous and sometimes fatal to the unwary.

A reasonably safe place to swim is one at which hazards are minimal. For example—
• The water should be clear and free from pollution.
• The bottom should slope gently toward deep water, and there should be no holes, sudden step-offs, or hidden obstructions such as large rocks, stumps, snags, and sunken logs.
• The bottom should be composed of firm sand, gravel, or shale— at least in standing-depth areas.
• There should be no silt, quicksand, shell patches, sharp and broken rock, or debris on the bottom.
• The area should be free of dangerous marine life or should be protected from it.
• Beach areas should be free of glass, shells, or debris that could cause injury to bare feet.
• Decks, piers, rafts, etc., should be of sturdy construction and should not be slippery.
• Swimming areas with strong currents or strong wave action should be avoided.

Nonswimmers require a considerable area of shallow water. They should not venture into water beyond shoulder depth. They should resist at all times the temptation to go beyond this depth with artificial supports such as air mattresses, inner tubes (Fig. 1), or beach balls or on the shoulders of a swimming companion. If the unexpected happens and the nonswimmer loses his support, the

FIG. 1

ability to regain the shore is also lost. Nonswimmers should not use flotation devices in any locations where they would not be comfortable and safe without them.

Weak or novice swimmers must confine their activities to areas in which they may be quickly and easily reached if anything goes wrong. They must be careful not to overestimate their ability. Good swimmers may venture more boldly than novices but they too must govern their activity by the application of good judgement and practical safety rules. They must remember that they are an ever-present example to the nonswimmer and novice alike, who seek to imitate their skill.

HAZARDS IN THE AQUATIC ENVIRONMENT

Although swimming is a pleasant and enjoyable experience, swimmers must be constantly alert to the hazards of the aquatic environment. Many of these dangers are inherent to the swimming area, while some stem from the swimmers themselves. Panic, exhaustion, and cramps are three conditions of personal danger. Anyone may be confronted by one or more of these conditions sometime in the aquatic experience and must be prepared to deal with them.

The action of the water and certain types of marine life present hazards to individuals who have not experienced open-water swimming as well as to those who frequent open-water sites. In supervised and well-regulated places, custom and knowledge of local conditions usually bring about the establishment of a set of regulations to govern the conduct and provide for the safety of swimmers. There are, however, some possibilities that accidents may occur despite observance of rules governing personal conduct. Such accidents arise from unforeseen circumstances and require some special knowledge of conditions and adaptation of skills to meet unusual situations.

Panic

Panic, a contributory cause in almost all water accidents, is a sudden unreasoning and overwhelming terror that destroys a person's capacity for self-help. Panic in the water is, of course, motivated by the fear of drowning and may be precipitated by such conditions as exhaustion, cramps, currents, and injuries from marine life. It most commonly attacks the nonswimmer and the novice, although the skilled swimmer is by no means immune. Persons who have learned to swim well and have prepared themselves for the hazards of the aquatic environment seldom panic. The tendency to panic should be steadfastly resisted, and all effort and thought should be given to removing one's self from the position or condition of danger.

Exhaustion

Another common contributory cause in water accidents is exhaustion. It is simply loss of energy and the resultant inability to make the necessary movements to keep afloat and make progress through the water. This condition may be brought about by entering the water when overtired from some prior physical activity, overexertion in swimming, reaction to cold water, or overestimation of one's ability. A person should not attempt to swim distances in deep water if safety is not within close reach. A swimmer can conserve energy and achieve relaxation by turning on the back and continuing to safety using a slow, relaxed, elementary backstroke. Another method of remaining afloat with a minimum of effort and energy is "survival floating"(see pages 163 through 166).

Cramps

Cramps occur in the muscles and are usually caused by fatigue, cold, or overexertion. While a person is swimming they occur most commonly in the foot, calf of the leg, or the hands. Occasionally, other muscles may cramp. The cramp causes the affected muscle to suddenly contract into a tight, hard knot, which incapacitates or greatly inhibits the movement of that muscle.

Although often painful, cramps are of little danger to swimmers unless they cause them to panic. Changing the stroke and relaxing will often bring relief. If the cramp continues, the swimmer should attempt to extend or stretch the muscle while applying pressure with the hand or hands. Frequently, a kneading or massaging action with the hands is helpful.

When the cramp is in the leg or foot, the swimmer should roll to a face-down position in the water, with lungs fully inflated, to extend and massage the affected muscle (Fig. 2). When the cramp is released, the person should swim to safety using a different movement of the affected part.

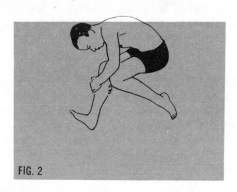

FIG. 2

Muscular cramps in the abdominal area, formerly attributed to overexertion too soon after eating, are not common, nor are they as extreme as formerly believed. If the swimmer does not panic and will relax, stretch, and change body position, it should be possible to stay afloat until the cramp is relieved or safety can be reached.

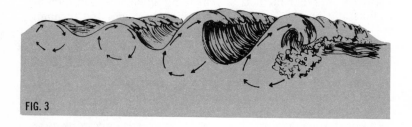

FIG. 3

Waves

From small lake ripples to huge ocean swells, waves are usually caused by the wind (Fig. 3). Waves may add to the enjoyment of swimming or may be disconcerting to those who do not understand their action. Persons swimming against an offshore breeze are often caught up in the illusion that the waves are running against them and carrying them out into deeper water. It should be noted that while wave motion travels, the water does not. Swimmers should fix their gaze upon some stationary object to convince themselves that they are making progress as they swim. Large, steep waves breaking close to shore are particularly dangerous to young children and the elderly, since the rushing, falling water can knock them from their feet and roll them about under the surface.

Currents

Currents, the flowing movement of a large volume of water seeking its own level, are an ever-present source of danger to river and open-water swimmers, since they tend to carry swimmers away from shore, often before they are aware of what is taking place.

River currents are most deceptive. They rarely follow the contour of the river bed, even in comparatively straight stretches, and are continually changing. Governed by projecting headlands, backwaters, islands, and the winding of the river's course, the river's direction of flow wanders from shore to shore. Eddies and reverse currents of varying intensity may be found near the riverbanks. The intensity of the current is based on volume of water and rate of riverbed drop.

Ocean currents are basically of two types, those caused by the tides and those caused by the runback of large waves from the shoreline. The risings and fallings of the water level due to tides are called tidal currents. As the tide "comes in," it creates the flood current, and as it "goes out," it becomes an ebb current. These regularly reversing patterns of water flow are not necessarily perpendicular to the shore. They may run diagonally or even parallel to the beach.

The backwash of waves, often called "undertow" (Fig. 4), is the force of water piled up by wave action receding down the slope of the beach back under the oncoming waves. The steepness of the incline and the volume of the water receding determine the intensity of the backwash. While the force of the backwash may knock the unwary from their feet and can be quite violent, it usually runs only a short distance.

Although there are many types of currents caused by tides, gravity, bottom contour, and wind, and many names for them, there is one fundamental principle that governs the safety of swimmers caught in a current: the current should never be

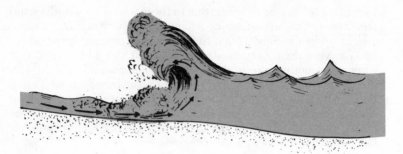

FIG. 4

"bucked." If the current has any strength, even the strongest
swimming effort cannot endure long. Good swimmers swim no
more than 3 miles an hour, and currents frequently run from 4 to 6
miles an hour. Swimmers should always swim diagonally across a
current and with its flow, even though they may come to shore some
distance from their entry point. This fact is particularly true of river

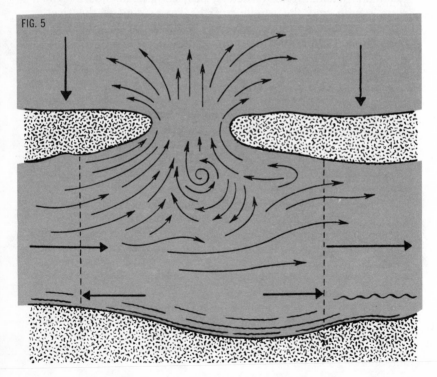

FIG. 5

and tidewater swimming, where currents run parallel to shore. When the direction of a current is straight outward from shore (Fig. 5), the swimmer caught in the current may need to swim with the current and diagonally across it until free from it, before being able to turn and return to shore.

Dangerous Marine Life

The natural aquatic environment teems with life, from plankton (small and microscopic plants and animals) to the baleen whale, largest of all animals. Man, relatively new to the aquatic environment, has frequently misrepresented the dangers of marine life. There is a need, however, to be wary in unfamiliar waters or when confronted with certain types of marine life.

Weeds

Water weeds, grass, and kelp are not a serious menace to the swimmer. There is a danger, however, to the inexperienced person who unknowingly dives or swims into a patch of weeds and becomes entangled. If the swimmer panics and attempts to convulsively thrash free, the weeds tend to wrap securely around the arms and legs. Slow, gentle, shaking and withdrawing movements of the limbs will serve to clear them, even though the first convulsive reaction at contact has bound the swimmer tightly. If there is a current, the swimmer should always go with it, since it will help to untangle and loosen the binding weeds. Water weeds such as kelp that float in a mass on the surface of the water may present a hazard to the swimmer who attempts to come to the surface under them. The swimmer should surface with hands over head and part the weeds. No attempt should be made to swim through the weeds. After getting the breath, the swimmer should look for a clear area, submerge, swim under the weeds, and continue this process until clear of danger.

Jellyfish and Portuguese Man-of-War

Jellyfish (Fig. 6A) and the Portuguese Man-of-War (Fig. 6B) occasionally plague some beach areas in large numbers. These umbrella-shaped, nearly transparent animals can grow as large as several feet in diameter. The tentacles of some varieties may cause reactions ranging from mild stings to violent reactions such as shock, cramps, nausea, and respiratory difficulty. Since tentacles may cling to the skin, the affected area should be wiped off with a towel or a handful of sand and then washed thoroughly with diluted ammonia or rubbing alcohol.

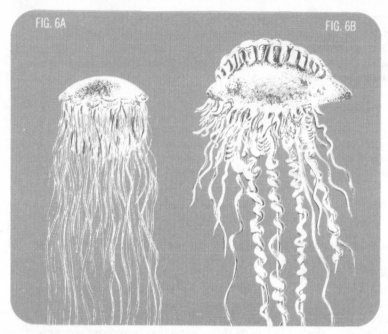

FIG. 6A   FIG. 6B

A medicine for the relief of pain, such as aspirin, should be given. If symptoms are severe, medical aid is needed. The swimmer should avoid contact with jellyfish both in the water and on the beach. If there is evidence of great numbers of jellyfish in the area, swimming is not advisable.

Cone Shells and Sea Urchins

The cone shell (Fig. 7A) is a type of mollusk related to the snail and has a complicated apparatus for injecting venom through a puncture wound. The general symptoms of cone shell poisoning include numbness and a tingling about the nose and mouth, paralysis, and even death from heart failure. Sea urchins are covered with sharp, brittle spines that frequently break off when they penetrate a hand or foot, and multiple venom organs (pedicellariae) containing a potent nerve poison. If a person is wounded by a cone shell or sea urchin, immediate soaking in hot water for 30 minutes, or use of hot compresses, may help to inactivate the venom. If symptoms are severe, the victim should seek medical aid.

Fire Coral

Fire coral (Fig. 7B), a smooth, mustard-yellow-color coral, injects

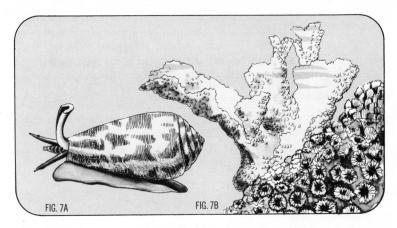

FIG. 7A   FIG. 7B

venom through stinging cells and produces multiple sharp cuts, which are contaminated by particles of broken-off calcareous (calcium-containing) material. These cuts require thorough cleaning, and the victim must have prompt medical assistance. Unless persons are protected by outergarments, gloves, and shoes, they should avoid areas near coral.

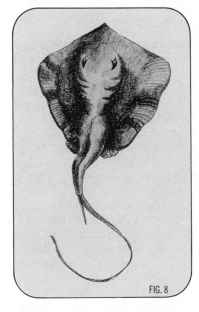

FIG. 8

Stingrays

Stingrays (Fig. 8) are normally very docile but can inflict a puncture wound and inject toxic venom from the barbed spines at the base of the tail. General symptoms of such a wound include shock, vomiting, diarrhea, and muscular paralysis. Medical assistance should be sought. In areas where stingrays may be, the swimmer should shuffle the feet through the sand when wading, since such movements normally frighten stingrays away.

Aquatic Predators

Sharks, barracudas, moray eels, and other predators all can produce severe bite wounds. First aid for wounds is covered in Chapter 12, Emergency First Aid. The best protection is not to swim in areas where aquatic predators are present.

SAFETY PRACTICES

Disregard or ignorance of good safety practices ranks high in the causes of drownings. Regardless of swimming ability, a person must follow personal safety practices to be safe in the aquatic environment.

Personal Water Safety

- Learn to swim well enough to survive in an emergency.
- Never swim alone and swim only with a "buddy" who has the ability to help when necessary.
- Swim only in supervised areas.
- Follow rules set up for the particular pool, beach, or waterfront where you are swimming.
- Learn the simple and safe reaching rescues.
- Know how to administer artificial resuscitation.
- Know your limitations and do not overestimate your ability.
- Stay out of the water when overheated and immediately after eating.
- Stay out of the water during electrical storms.
- Dive only into known waters of sufficient depth.
- Do not substitute inflated tubes, air mattresses, or other artificial supports for swimming ability.
- Always swim a safe distance away from diving boards and platforms.
- Avoid long periods of immersion and overexposure to the sun.
- Take instruction under qualified instructors before participating in such aquatic sports as skin and scuba diving and water-skiing.
- Call for help only when you really need it.

Safety at Home Pools

- Never permit anyone to swim alone. Constant and responsible supervision is a must. Never leave a child unattended in the pool area, even for the length of time it takes to answer a telephone or the front door.
- See that the pool has adequate fencing and a gate with a lock to prevent children from unauthorized entry.
- Keep basic rescue and lifesaving equipment readily available.
- Post emergency instructions and emergency telephone numbers conspicuously.
- Have an adequate first aid kit available.
- Enforce common-sense safety rules at all times. Make sure that at least one responsible person knows how to administer artificial respiration and give proper first aid.
- Clearly mark the deep and shallow sections. Mark the separation of deep and shallow water by use of a buoyed line whenever weak swimmers or nonswimmers are using the pool.
- Do not allow running, pushing, or boisterous play on the deck.
- Encourage responsible parents or other adults to give water safety and swimming instruction to youngsters. (A recommended text is the American Red Cross booklet *Teaching Johnny To Swim*.)
- Make sure there is adequate filtration to maintain good clarity of the water. Consult the local health department for regulations on pool sanitation.
- Do not allow pool users to bring bottles, glasses, and sharp objects to the pool area.
- Observe applicable personal safety rules.

Safety at Farm Ponds

- Never swim alone.
- Mark off safe swimming areas with buoyed lines. Remove underwater snags, bottles, and debris.
- Avoid swimming in areas immediately in front of steep-sloping banks.
- Post warning signs at danger points.
- Supervise children at all times.
- Have water checked and approved by the local health department and recheck it periodically if it is used for swimming.
- If practical, erect an adequate fence and a gate with a lock to prevent unauthorized entry into the pond area by children.
- Keep basic rescue and lifesaving equipment readily available.
- Post emergency instructions and emergency telephone numbers conspicuously.

- Have an adequate first aid kit available.
- Enforce common-sense safety rules. Make sure that at least one responsible person knows how to administer artificial respiration, perform basic reaching rescues, and give proper first aid.
- Have a responsible adult start water safety and swimming instruction for children who are potential farm pond users. (A recommended text is the American Red Cross booklet *Teaching Johnny To Swim.*)
- Make sure that piers, rafts, and landings are well built and securely braced.
- Observe applicable personal safety rules.
- If a pond is used for skating, add a ladder to the safety post as helpful emergency ice rescue equipment. Maintain supervision at all times.
- To avoid accidents on the ice, never skate alone, skate only on a safe thickness of ice, and skate only in a restricted area.

Safety at Beaches

- Swim in areas supervised by a lifeguard.
- Never swim alone.
- Check with a lifeguard regarding beach and surf conditions before swimming.
- Report any unsafe beach condition to the lifeguard.
- If caught in a current, swim with it and diagonally across it until you are freed.
- Call or wave for help if unable to swim out of a strong current.
- Never fake trouble or calls for help.
- Never substitute the use of floating devices for swimming ability.
- Do not use breakable objects on the beach, and if any are found, pick them up and dispose of them for your own protection and the safety of others.
- Do not dive into unknown water or into shallow, breaking waves.
- Do not overestimate your ability by attempting long-distance swims unless swimming parallel to shore and within easy reach of safety.
- Supervise small children even when lifeguards are on duty.
- Do not swim close to piers or pilings.
- Do not throw sand or engage in any kind of horseplay.
- Avoid dangerous marine life.
- Do not engage in unnecessary conversation with a lifeguard.
- Observe applicable personal safety rules.
- Respect the judgment and experience of the trained lifeguards, follow their advice, and do not interfere with the performance of their duty.

2

SAFETY AND RESCUE EQUIPMENT

The availability of selected safety and rescue equipment should be a vital requirement at all swimming areas, although not all of the equipment described here is necessary for every facility. All equipment should be kept in good, usable condition, and all personnel should be trained in its proper use.

- *Lifelines*—These are buoyed lines (Fig. 9) that mark and separate swimming and diving area limits. In an emergency, they can afford temporary support to a tired swimmer.

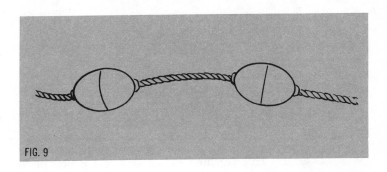

FIG. 9

- *Booms*—These are made of good-sized logs chained together and are often used to enclose an entire swimming area, especially in streams and rivers. They serve as a breakwater and, in an emergency, offer support and protection.
- *Ring buoy*—The ring buoy (a throwable device) is considered as standard equipment at pools and beaches. The 18″-diameter buoy (Fig. 10) is made of solid, buoyant plastic and weighs about 2½ pounds. The grab line and the 50-foot retrieving line are made of ¼-inch polyutherene line with a "lemon" on the free end. The buoy meets specifications as a U.S. Coast Guard approved "throwable" personal flotation device (PFD). When properly mounted, the buoy is hung over the top spindle with the line over the lower spindle, and the device should always be ready for instant use in an emergency.

FIG. 10

- *Shepherd's crook*—This reaching device (Fig. 11) is one of the oldest known pieces of pool rescue equipment. The blunted hook is large enough to encircle the entire body of the victim and is effective even though the victim may be unconscious and unable to hold on. The use of lightweight aluminum has made this formerly unwieldy equipment far more effective and usable.

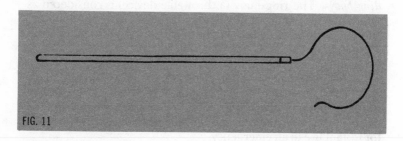

FIG. 11

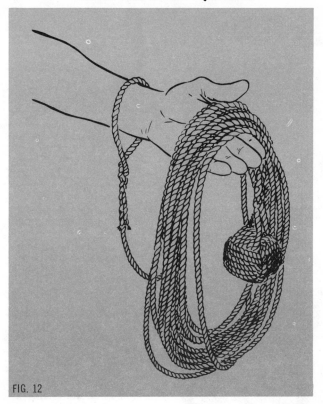

FIG. 12

- *Heaving line*—Any strong line, properly coiled (Fig. 12) and thrown, can be used to extend the rescuer's reach to 30 or 40 feet. Because lines are lightweight, they are most effective if they have a large knot or a "monkey fist" on the throwing end.
- *Safety post*—A homemade safety post (Fig. 13) can be constructed from easily obtainable materials and should be set near water at any point where swimmers might get into difficulty. The 4-inch-by-4-inch post should be set 2 feet into the ground and have a metal shelf bracket or a 60-penny spike about 1 foot from the top as a hook for coiled rope and a plastic jug. A 40-foot length of line should be tied securely to the handle of a gallon plastic jug containing an inch or so of water for weight in throwing. At the other end of the line, a 4-inch piece of 2 by 2 should be fastened to prevent line from slipping completely through the hands, or from underfoot, when thrown. A 10-foot or 12-foot bamboo pole, for reaching assists, may be secured down through two 6-

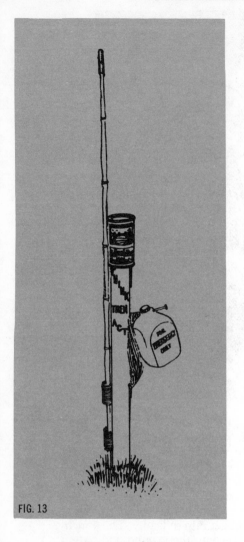

FIG. 13

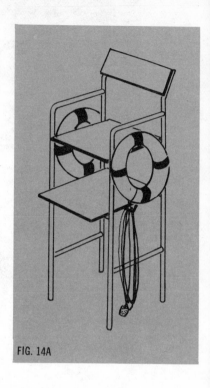

FIG. 14A

ounce cans nailed near the bottom of the post. A poster on safety tips may be attached to a metal or plastic container and inverted over the top of the post (see Red Cross safety post Poster, Poster 1021).

- *Lifeguard stands*—These stands, although constructed to suit individual facilities, should meet some general specifications. They should be from 5 to 6 feet above deck level and should have proper foot and back rests, with some provision made for shade

FIG. 14B

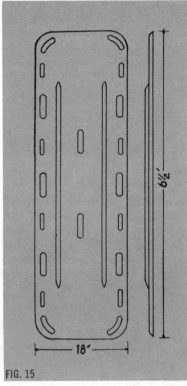

FIG. 15

and shelter. They should include some sort of hooks or supports for safety equipment such as either a reaching pole or a ring buoy with line, or both, or a rescue tube. Most pool guard stands (Fig. 14A) are made of stainless steel pipe set into the pool deck. Lakefronts are often equipped with wooden structures built on pilings or affixed to piers. Suitable, safe ladders for mounting are recommended. On beaches where tides cause significant changes in water level, portable chairs or stands (Fig. 14B) may be used. Beach stands should be wide enough to comfortably seat two guards and should have provision made for torpedo buoy and line or rescue tube, in addition to first aid equipment.

- *Backboards*—Backboards (Fig. 15), or spine boards, should be standard rescue equipment at all swimming facilities. A backboard can be easily made from inexpensive materials, varnished with several coats of a good spar varnish, and should be kept readily available. Exterior or marine ¾-inch plywood, 18 inches by 6½ feet, should be rounded at the corners and equipped with hand and tie-down holes. Narrow wooden "runners" glued to the underside facilitate lifting from deck areas. Some backboards are equipped with permanently affixed tie-down straps. If paint, rather than varnish, is desired, nonmetalic paint should be used.

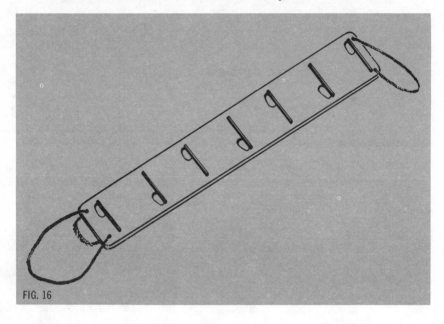

FIG. 16

- *"Allaboard"*—The "Allaboard" (Fig. 16) is an effective safety and rescue device for a variety of aquatic situations. Constructed of 1-inch marine plywood, the 8-foot-by-16-inch board has hand and foot holes, 5 inches by 2½ inches, with wooden cleats, ¾ inch by ¾ inch by 10 inches, flush with the base of each hole. A loop of line is attached to each end. The board is varnished on one side and fiberglassed on the other side for added strength.
- *Rescue tubes*—These excellent rescue devices (Fig. 17) are made of vinyl foam, approximately 3 inches by 6 inches by 40 inches, and come complete with a 6-foot-long polyethylene towline and a web shoulder strap.
- *Folding canvas stretchers*—The standard army-type folding stretcher (Fig. 18) should be available at poolside for emergency transportation. Proper use of such equipment should be a part of in-service first aid training for guards.
- *Rescue boards*—Because of the speed with which it can be propelled through the water, the rescue board (Fig. 19) is an

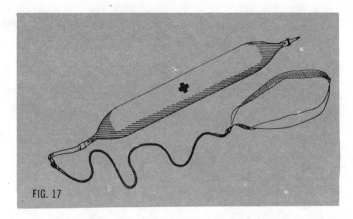

FIG. 17

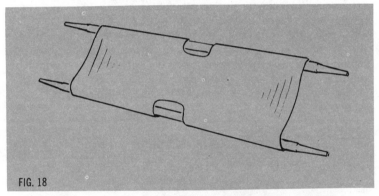

FIG. 18

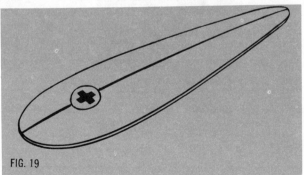

FIG. 19

excellent rescue device in the hands of a trained user. The board is approximately 10 feet by 22 inches by 4 inches and is made of fiberglass, balsa, or marine plywood. The boards usually weigh from 50 to 75 pounds.

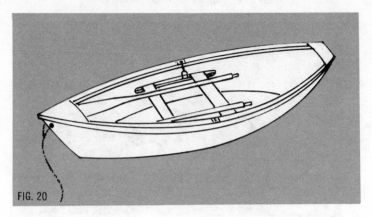

FIG. 20

- *Lifeboats*—Powerboats and rowboats (Fig. 20) used for life-saving and rescue should be equipped with extra oars, a throwing ring buoy, a 25-foot heaving line, a reaching pole, an anchor, a bailer, and a first aid kit. Extra oars should be lashed inside the boat, and provision should be made for keeping first aid equipment dry. A Coast Guard approved personal floatation device (PED) is required for each occupant.

FIG. 21

- *Whistles*—If properly used, the whistle is a valuable piece of safety equipment. Chrome-plated brass whistles are generally used, since their sharp, penetrating tone carries well. Some plastic whistles are equally suitable. The whistle (Fig. 21) is ordinarily secured to a strong lanyard worn around the neck.

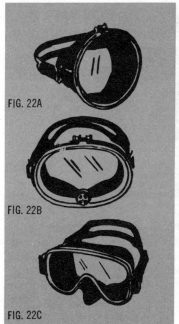

FIG. 22A

FIG. 22B

FIG. 22C

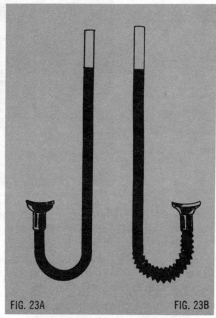

FIG. 23A   FIG. 23B

- *Face masks*—Masks should be constructed of soft, flexible rubber with an untinted, shatterproof, safety glass facepiece (Fig. 22A), held in position by a corrosion-proof metal band. A single or a divided strap holds the mask in place and can be adjusted to fit the wearer. Some masks are equipped with a purge valve (Fig. 22B), which allows the individual to clear water from the mask by exhaling through the nose. Masks with a nose-blocking device (Fig. 22C), or with a molded indentation to fit the nose, enable the swimmer to block off or pinch the nose to equalize air pressure in the ear canal as the swimmer dives more deeply.
- *Fins*—Swim fins are constructed in various ways. Some float, others do not. Some are designed with a full foot, others are open at the heel and are held in position by a heel strap. Fins should be individually selected for proper fit, flexibility, and blade size.
- *Snorkels*—These are J-shaped rubber tubes from 12 to 15 inches in length. Some are molded in one piece (Fig. 23A), while others have a ribbed, flexible section (Fig. 23B) for the curved portion of the tube. All are fitted with a soft, rubber, flanged mouthpiece, which should be the right size for the user, to prevent water seeping in as the person breathes.

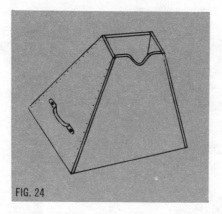

FIG. 24

- *Aquascope* —This piece of equipment is of value for scanning the bottom where waters are relatively clear and shallow. These devices (Fig. 24) can be used effectively at night in combination with a powerful flashlight. The aquascope is being replaced in many areas by the use of mask, fins, and snorkel, which make possible a more rapid search.

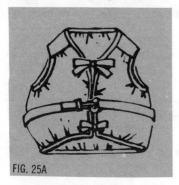

FIG. 25A

FIG. 25B

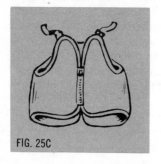

FIG. 25C

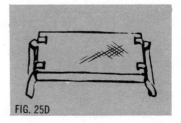

FIG. 25D

- *Personal flotation devices (PFD's)* —Coast Guard approved personal flotation devices are required by law aboard all small craft, including lifeguard boats. In addition, use of such equipment should be taught in instructional swimming programs. The life preserver (Fig. 25A), buoyant vest (Fig. 25B), and special-purpose vest (Fig. 25C) are examples of U.S. Coast Guard approved wearable personal flotation devices. The buoyant cushion (Fig. 25D) and the ring lifebuoy (Fig. 25E) are examples of throwable devices. Care should be taken to select only those devices bearing the U.S. Coast Guard approval seal.

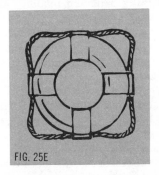

FIG. 25E

3

NONSWIMMING AND EQUIPMENT RESCUES

Elementary forms of rescue constitute the safest and most effective methods of assisting a person in difficulty without exposing the rescuer to unnecessary dangers. Because of the many risks involved, only a swimmer who has been trained and has mastered lifesaving techniques should attempt a swimming rescue.

Not even the trained lifesaver should attempt to rescue a victim without maintaining a position of safety. This position can be on shore, pier, or deck, or on some type of craft. Since actual contact with a victim can be dangerous and often is unnecessary, the rescue can usually be effected by reaching, extending the reach, or using a boat. When it is necessary to actually swim to the victim, some type of basic rescue equipment or any buoyant object should be used and extended to the victim while the rescuer is still out of reach.

REACHING RESCUES

In a reaching rescue, the rescuer lies flat on the deck of the pool (Fig. 26) or on a pier, with body anchored and securely braced, and extends a hand to the victim. The rescuer grasps the victim's wrist from above and then draws the victim slowly and carefully to safety.

If the victim is beyond arm's reach from the lying position, the rescuer can quickly slip into the water (Fig. 27) and, while firmly hanging onto a support with one hand, reach out with a free hand and pull the victim to safety.

If the victim is beyond arm's reach in the water, the rescuer's legs may be extended to the victim (Fig. 28), while the rescuer maintains a firm grasp on the pool ladder, overflow trough, piling, etc.

While attempting a reaching rescue, the rescuer should keep talking in an effort to calm and instruct the victim.

Improvised Equipment for Reaching Rescues

When the victim is beyond arm's reach or body extension, the rescuer may use a towel or an item of clothing such as a belt, shirt, or coat. Other readily available items that can be used for extending are a paddle, an oar, a pole, or a branch.

FIG. 26

FIG. 27

FIG. 28

FIG. 29

Shepherd's Crook

The shepherd's crook is a long, light, aluminum pole with a blunted hook that is large enough to encircle a person's body (Fig. 29). It is usually hung on a rack or on hooks at a convenient location at a point where it is likely to be needed. The hook end can be quickly placed around the victim's chest, under the armpits, and is especially useful when a victim is unconscious or unable to grasp an extended rescue device. The rescuer keeps firmly braced and slowly pulls the victim to safety.

WADING RESCUES OR ASSISTS

When a victim is beyond the extended reach, a human chain may be used if several people are present (Fig. 30A). The rescuers enter the water and form a chain, with each grasping the wrist of the person on either side in a wrist-to-wrist grip (Fig. 30B) and with every other rescuer facing in the same direction. The chain is lengthened by the individuals' extending their arms as they wade out. When the victim is contacted, the chain is drawn back to shore by each person in turn, starting by having the anchor person nearest shore pull the next person in the chain to him.

In current or rushing streams, the human chain should be formed on shore, and after the chain enters the water, the lightest person generally should be the one farthest out in the water.

FIG. 30A

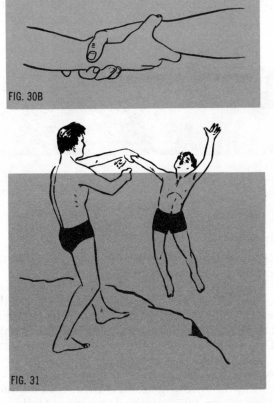

FIG. 30B

FIG. 31

A lone wader may advance into the water only to about chest depth with comparative safety. The rescuer should lean back shoreward before reaching down from above to grasp the victim (Fig. 31). In deeper waters, the rescuer must guard against being pulled out before starting to pull in the victim. As in reaching assists, extending a pole, branch, or article of clothing would be a safer method of assisting the victim.

USE OF FREE-FLOATING SUPPORT

The wader may avoid personal contact in making an assist by using a plank (Fig. 32), kickboard, buoyant cushion, or other similar buoyant object. The rescuer can then wade to a point near the victim but still remain safe so that the floating object can be pushed to reach the victim. The victim can then be encouraged to hang onto the object and kick toward safety.

FIG. 32

THROWING ASSISTS

Heaving Line

A coiled length of line can be hung conveniently in place at swimming areas and makes an excellent rescue device. Before the line is thrown, one end of it should be looped around one of the rescuer's wrists or be secured by being stepped on with the forward foot (Fig. 35A). The coiled line is hung over the palm of the hand, and this hand is extended forward at waist level. The coil should be split so that about half of the coil is in each hand. This action gives the coil in the throwing hand sufficient weight so that it can be thrown with some accuracy.

The coil in the throwing hand is thrown in an underhand motion (Fig. 33), and the extended line should fall just beyond the shoulder of the victim and within reach of the victim's outstretched hands. The palm of the nonthrowing hand is kept open to allow the coil to run freely.

A heaving line can be thrown with better accuracy if it is

FIG. 33

weighted. The weight should be attached to the end that is thrown and preferably should be buoyant. A monkey-fist makes a suitable weighted device.

Heaving Jug

A suitable piece of rescue equipment can be made from a gallon plastic container, to which has been added about ½ inch of water. The container can be attached to a length of line, and the container and coil of line can be hung conveniently in place at swimming areas. Before the equipment is thrown, the rescuer should secure the nonthrowing end either with a loop around the wrist or by placing the forward foot on the line near the nonthrowing end. The coil of line is hung over the palm of one hand, and the throw is made by grasping the handle of the jug and releasing it at the forward end of a pendulum swing (Fig. 34). Getting a firm grasp on the buoyant jug, the victim can be hauled in hand over hand. Care should be taken to pull fast enough to keep the victim's head above water but smoothly enough so that the jug is not jerked from the victim's grasp.

Ring Buoy and Line

A ring buoy with line attached is available at many swimming areas and can be a valuable piece of rescue equipment. The ring

FIG. 34

buoy for heaving purposes should weigh about 2½ pounds and should be made of a buoyant material such as cork, kapok, foam rubber, or solid plastic. Attached should be 50 feet of ¼-inch manila or polyethylene line. The other end of the line should have a wooden or plastic "lemon" or a wrist loop. The ring buoy should be hung where it will not be blown off the hook on which it rests and should be positioned at a height where anybody can easily seize both it and the coil of line hung directly below it.

The rescuer should hold the ring buoy with the throwing hand grasping over and down on the side farthest from the body, fingers holding the bottom side directly opposite where the line is attached. The foot farthest from the buoy is placed forward, across the end of the line in front of the "lemon." The coiled line hangs over the extended and open nonthrowing hand so that the line pays off and over the fingertips (Fig. 35A).

The throw is normally an underhand toss, with the buoy aimed just beyond the victim (Fig. 35B). After the victim has a firm grasp on the buoy or grab line, the rescuer, using a steady pull, hauls the victim (Fig. 35C) to safety, being careful not to jerk the buoy out of the victim's grip.

In a wind, the throw should be to windward, not in a direct line to the victim, so that the drift will bring the buoy to the victim's reach. If the throw is inaccurate, the line may be pulled in to the hand that

FIG. 35A

FIG. 35B

FIG. 35C

held the coiled line. The rescuer should stand sideways to the line in the water. The throwing hand should grasp the line, fingers down, on the far side of the line, with the little finger toward the buoy. With the rescuer alternately pulling the line to the other hand and sliding out to get more line, recoiling may be done in orderly fashion just as quickly as by pulling in the line with both hands. The next throw can then be made with less possibility of fouling the line.

If distance, inaccuracy, or the prevailing condition of the wind places the buoy out of reach of the victim, the rescuer must quickly decide what alternative exists. If the thrower is a non-swimmer or a poor swimmer, there is little choice other than to draw in the line and try again. If, however, the rescuer is a capable swimmer or has had some lifesaving training, the safest alternative is to swim out to the buoy. When within arm's reach of the victim, the rescuer should then push the buoy to the victim (Fig. 36). After the victim has a firm grasp on the buoy (Fig. 37), the rescuer can tow the victim to safety by grasping the attached line well out of reach of the victim. Talking and giving instructions to the victim will usually help to keep the individual calm and under control.

FIG. 36

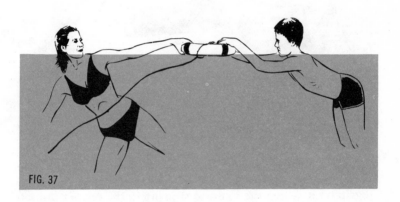

FIG. 37

RESCUE USING SPARE AUTO TIRE

An automobile spare tire that is inflated and mounted on a wheel can make an excellent piece of rescue equipment in an emergency. It can be easily rolled down a beach incline and then pushed ahead of the rescuer. Pushing the spare tire out to the victim is facilitated by pressing down slightly on the tire at the point where the rescuer has hand contact (Fig. 38). This action will raise the opposite side of the tire, thereby lessening the resistance as the tire moves against the water. Several people can easily be supported by a spare tire

FIG. 38

FIG. 39

when it is inflated to its normal pressure. To make it easier for the victim to grasp the tire, it can be dipped so that the victim can get a grip on it. When the victim is supported, the rescuer can safely begin to tow to shore (Fig 39).

SWIMMING RESCUE BY UNTRAINED SWIMMER

If a person is in danger of drowning only a short distance from shore and there is no rescue equipment of any kind available, the untrained swimmer may feel that it is necessary to attempt the rescue. In such cases, the rescuer should swim to a position behind the victim and make contact with the victim by seizing the person's hair (Fig. 40). The rescuer should then turn on the side and stroke hard to regain the shore. If little or no progress is made or if the rescuer is in danger of being grabbed by the victim, the novice rescuer can always let go and swim out of reach.

FIG. 40

FIG. 41

POOL RESCUE BY UNTRAINED SWIMMER

In a pool situation, and only when there is no rescue equipment available, an untrained swimmer may attempt a rescue by jumping or diving to a position behind and below the victim (Fig. 41). The rescuer can then grasp the victim at the waist or thighs and, while supporting the victim, walk or push the person to safety at the side of the pool.

SURFBOARD RESCUES

The original surfboard was designed by the Hawaiians hundreds of years ago as a solid board weighing hundreds of pounds. Boards varied in length, but the average size was about 12 feet. With the advent of the hollow-type and balsa boards in the 1920's, surfboards became light enough to be easily launched and paddled and could be used as a piece of rescue equipment by one rescuer. These boards varied in length up to 14 feet, depending on the type and purpose for which they were to be used.

The modern boards are generally made of fiberglass and are of two types. The rescue board is at least 10 feet long and about 22 inches wide and is buoyant enough to support the weight of two adults. The surfboard varies from 6 to 8 feet in length, is flat on the bottom, has a bottom fin, and has only enough buoyancy to support one person. It is not adaptable for rescue; however, in an emergency it is useful in getting to a victim quickly and effecting a rescue by providing support for the victim.

To use a board for rescue, the rescuer should be thoroughly skilled in paddling and maneuvering the board. A rescuer's ability to make rescues will depend upon the extent of the rescuer's skill in the various methods and conditions of rescue to which the board is adapted. Handling and rescue skills should be perfected in quiet waters before a person attempts to use a rescue board in surf or rough water.

Launching the Board

The simplest method of launching is to place the board in the water at about knee depth, hold onto the sides about midway, run, and push the board. Without checking momentum, the rescuer jumps on the board, landing in a position similar to a three-point pushup position. The rescuer adjusts balance, lowers the body gently, and starts paddling.

If the rescuer has enough strength and skill, the quicker launching method may be attempted. The rescuer holds the board just as a person would hold a sled. The individual runs into the water until ankle depth is reached, then crouches, and drops the board somewhat forward and flat on the surface. Without losing momentum, the rescuer then quickly jumps onto the board, adjusts position, lowers the body, and paddles out toward the victim.

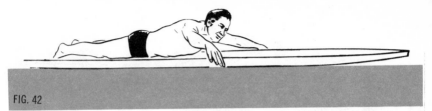

FIG. 42

Approaching

In quiet waters, the rescuer should simply point the board toward the victim and paddle, using either the crawl arm action or the butterfly arm action (Fig. 42). The head should be up, and the eyes should be on the victim. The shoulders must be up off the board so that the rescuer can attain effective paddling action.

For approaching through surf, the rescuer must apply three basic principles: the board must always be kept at right angles to the waves; the board must have sufficient momentum to get past the "breaks"; the paddler must use good judgment and knowledge in selecting the spot to go through and in timing the action of the surf.

Moderate waves can be ridden through by proper timing. Just as the wave crests in front of the board, the rescuer does a pushup, holding tightly to the sides of the board and allowing the crest or white water to pass between the board and the rescuer's raised body.

When large waves are about to break on the rescuer, the paddler should flatten out on the board, head down, and hold tight, with hands extended, somewhat forward against the sides.

When an extra-large wave is about to break, it may be necessary for the rescuer to drop over the side of the board, duck under the foam as much as possible, and turn the board on edge to lessen resistance. In this position, the board should be held securely against the rescuer's body.

Rescue of Tired Swimmer

When rescuing a tired swimmer, the rescuer approaches the victim from either side, paddling in a prone position. The rescuer grasps the victim's nearest hand or wrist (Fig. 43) and sits up as soon as contact is made. The drag of the victim's body and the resistance caused by the action of the rescuer's legs in sitting up will stop the board's forward progress. The rescuer's feet and lower legs in the water stabilize the board, and additional stabilization can be achieved by the rescuer's performing a rotary, or "eggbeater," kick.

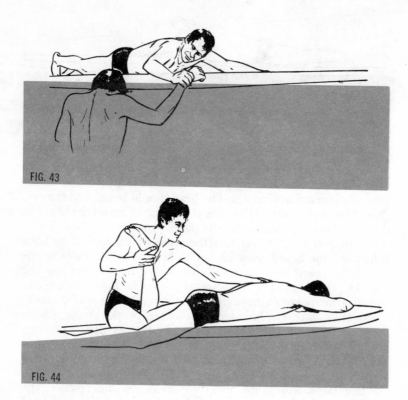

FIG. 43

FIG. 44

The victim's arms are extended across the board and in the resting position, and the victim can be encouraged to relax and rest until calmed down. The method of getting the victim on the board will depend on the person's condition. The victim may be able to climb aboard without help or may need assistance. While the victim has been in the resting position, the rescuer should have turned the board toward shore prior to having the victim get aboard. The victim gets aboard by staying low and swimming onto the board in front of the still-seated rescuer (Fig. 44). With the victim then in a prone lying position, the rescuer lies down between the victim's spread legs, chest riding on victim's thighs. The rescuer adjusts both his and the victim's positions so that the bow, or tip, of the board is up high enough to clear the water.

The rescuer's legs can be spread and used as outriggers in the water for added stability. The return to shore should be unhurried, and the rescuer should be alert to spot lulls in the surf when approaching the beach.

If the victim cannot climb onto the board without help, the rescuer places the victim's arms across the board. The rescuer gets the victim up into a horizontal position by pushing up with the foot under the victim's body. The rescuer then carefully and slowly drags the victim onto the board. The rescuer should fold the victim's arms to act as protection and as a cushion for the head (Fig. 45). The approach to shore is slow and controlled, with the rescuer using a crawl stroke arm action for propulsion.

FIG. 45

Rescue of Panicky Victim

The rescuer contacts the panicky victim as described in the rescue of a tired swimmer. As the victim's wrist is grabbed, the rescuer slides off the board, capsizing it at the same time (Fig. 46). The rescuer is then still holding the victim's wrist across the board, with the board between the rescuer and the victim (Fig. 47). At this point, the victim should be calmed and made to understand how assistance will be given and what action will be expected of the victim.

Prior to getting the victim onto the board, the board should be turned and pointed toward shore. The victim's forearms are placed on the board, with the rescuer maintaining contact. The rescuer reaches across the board and rolls the board back to its upright position (Fig. 48), thereby rolling the victim across and onto the board. The rescuer mounts the board, rotates the victim (still in a prone position) so that the victim's head is toward the bow (Fig. 49), adjusts both positions for proper balance, assumes the paddling position, and starts for shore (Fig. 50).

FIG. 46

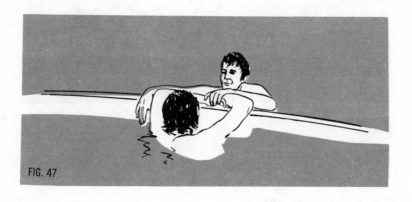

FIG. 47

FIG. 48

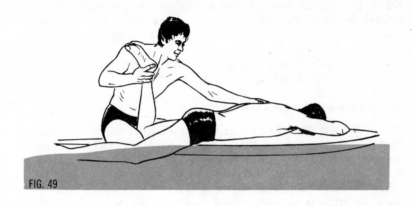

FIG. 49

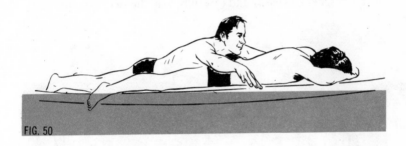

FIG. 50

Rescue Using One-Man Surfboard

In an emergency, the pleasure surfboard could be used with modifications of the technique. The rescuer goes out through the breakers as described with the rescue board. After making contact with the victim, the rescuer holds the victim in a resting position, with arms across the board, and signals for assistance. If the victim needs more support, the rescuer can slip off the board and assist the victim to a prone resting position. The board should have been turned toward shore, and if no help is forthcoming, the surfboard with the victim aboard can be slowly and carefully pushed to shore.

RESCUE TUBE

The rescue tube is a vinyl foam, free-floating support that can easily be towed to a victim. It has sufficient buoyancy to support one or more victims and is an indispensable piece of rescue equipment for surf or rough water. It has all the advantages of the metal torpedo buoy plus the fact that it is flexible, can be wrapped around a victim or the rescuer, and has no sharp or hard edges. It is rapidly replacing the metal buoy. The rescue tube was designed and originally used at Southern California surf beaches, but its use has now spread to the East Coast beaches.

Use of Tube as Throwable Device

If a victim is struggling in the water no farther than 6 or 8 feet from safety, the ends of the rescue tube can be quickly clasped together, making an improvised ring buoy. The rescuer can throw the tube with one hand and hold onto the webbing loop with the other (Fig. 51). Since the towline is 6 feet long and the webbed shoulder strap is an additional 2 feet long, a simple and quick rescue could be made in this manner. When the victim grasps the tube, the rescuer can easily and carefully haul the victim to safety.

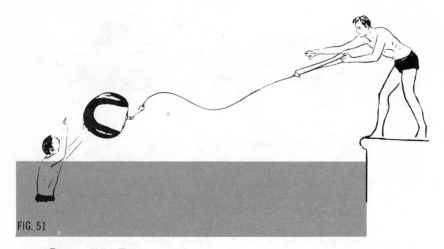

FIG. 51

Rescue With Tube

In most cases, the rescue tube is used initially without a trail line attached to shore. The rescuer grasps the tube in one hand and loops the webbed shoulder strap over one shoulder (Fig. 52) and under the opposite arm. How the rescuer enters the water will depend on the circumstances. If necessary to enter from an elevated pier, the rescuer can make a "stride jump" (Fig. 53). Letting the tube free in midair, the rescuer immediately starts stroking toward the victim.

FIG. 52

FIG. 53

FIG. 54

FIG. 55

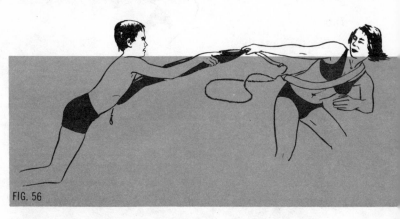

FIG. 56

At a beach, the rescuer would make a "run and plunge" entry. Carrying the tube in one hand, the rescuer runs into the water, lifting the feet as high as possible in each stride in order to clear the water (Fig. 54). At the point where running through deepening water becomes slower, the rescuer takes a shallow forward dive while letting go of the tube and swims toward the victim, keeping eye contact with the victim. Upon reaching a point within about 5 or 6 feet of the victim, the rescuer stops and extends the tube to the victim (Fig. 55). If the victim is excited or panicky, the rescuer may slip out of the shoulder loop to insure not being drawn to the victim. After calming the victim, the rescuer can tow the person to safety by hanging onto the strap at the end of the tube (Fig. 56). Depending on the equipment and the help available, the rescuer may signal for help in the form of another rescuer or signal for a trail line that could be snapped in place so that the victim can be towed to shore.

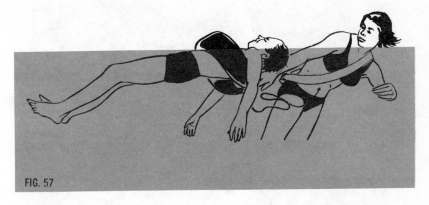

FIG. 57

Tube Clasped Around Victim

The tube can be used even if the rescuer determines that the victim might not have sufficient strength to hang onto it. After reaching the victim, the rescuer may wrap the tube around the victim, clasp the tube ends together with the metal loop and latch, roll the victim onto the back position, and tow the victim in (Fig. 57). In surf, the buoyancy provided is sufficient so that the rescuer can gauge the breakers and keep the victim's face above the water.

Tube Clasped Around Rescuer

Another method that can be used without the victim's hanging onto the tube is for the rescuer to clasp the tube around his own upper body. The rescuer can then make the desired approach, make contact, and tow the victim to shore using a cross-chest (Fig. 58), hair, or armpit tow, depending on choice and circumstances.

FIG. 58

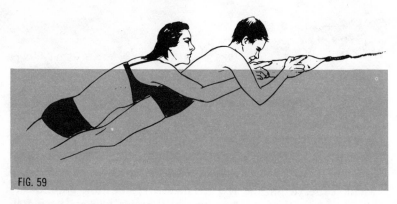

FIG. 59

Rescue With Trail Line Attached

When a victim is towed to shore with trail line attached, the victim seizes the tube and slides the head and chest about halfway up the tube, hanging onto the sides. The rescuer slides to the rear and takes a similar position, reaching under the victim's arm to get a handhold on the sides of the tube (Fig. 59). When ready, the rescuer signals to shore, and both rescuer and victim are hauled to safety.

4

WATER RESCUES

Only when all other less hazardous ways of rescuing a drowning person are impossible should anyone consider the idea of swimming after the victim. What rescue procedure to use will depend upon the condition of the victim, of the rescuer, and of the environment. The greater the skill, training, and experience on the part of the potential rescuer, the greater the chance of a successful outcome when attempting a swimming rescue.

CONDITIONS AFFECTING RESCUE

Condition of Victim

How much time may pass before the drowning person becomes unconscious may be gauged by noticing (1) whether the victim is frightened and panicky, not in immediate danger of becoming unconscious, (2) whether the victim flutters the arms briefly and loses buoyancy within a few seconds, or (3) whether almost immediately, without visible flurry, the victim loses the air he exchanges and sinks toward the bottom.

The size of the victim can sometimes cause difficulty. Buoyancy of a body is likely to be little if the victim is lean and big-boned. Other types of bodies have a fair degree of buoyancy. Some types have marginal buoyancy. Still others have no buoyancy at all. On the other hand, a body with much fatty tissue will have great buoyancy and will be easy to handle in the water. These characteristics are not controlled by size alone.

Condition of Rescuer

Restraint upon emotions must be exercised by anyone who attempts to prevent loss of life due to drowning. The immediate and natural impulse is to respond by taking the last-resort course of action first. Training and knowledge mean experience. They bring a clear realization to anybody about what can and cannot be done to rescue a drowning person. Training should include practice in the rescue of a variety of victims: large and small, light and heavy, actively struggling and passive, etc.

Learning and practicing the techniques for each situation will give the discipline that produces the right response to an emergency need. Experience will tell rescuers how far they can safely go out into the water and come back and how much of a load they can bear. It will, in addition, tell them how much time they have to get stricken persons back conscious and breathing or to recover an unconscious, nonbreathing person who may still be revived. At times, in cool objectivity, the witness to an occurring drowning will have to decide against a swimming rescue attempt. It is better that one rather than two drown.

Conditions of Environment

The chances of making a successful swimming rescue are reduced by strong winds, large waves, violent currents, poor vision above and below the water, plant growth, dangerous creatures in the water, and low temperatures. The fury of a wild sea would make the thought of a swimming rescue ridiculous. The victim could not be seen, and the rescuer would have to be extremely lucky if he or she were able to return to a boat or shore, even if it were possible to reach the victim. At best, a small-boat rescue might be made, but it would involve great risk in these circumstances.

In making a swimming rescue in an area where plant growth abounds, the rescuer must avoid fast movements, which might cause binding entanglement. Only smooth, easy swimming strokes would allow successful penetration of the plant area. That means greatly reduced speed.

The depth to which a rescuer may go to retrieve the victim will depend upon how long the breath can be held after swimming to the site and upon the depth itself. The rescuer can prevent damage to the ears as the descent is made by strongly blowing the nose while holding the air from escaping. This action causes pressure to balance back against external pressure.

SWIMMING RESCUE

The rescuer is confronted with a number of decisions that must be made that could affect either the rescuer's life or the victim's—or both. From start to finish, a swimming rescue is made up of a series of skills: takeoffs, approach stroking, safe contact with the victim, selection of the best type of carry or assist to take the person to safety, possibly the application of artificial respiration, and, finally, the decision of how best to remove the victim from the water.

Takeoffs

Since it is advisable to keep an eye on a victim and to make sure of the victim's position if the victim should sink below the surface, it is usually best to take off in one of the following ways.

Stride Jump

In the stride jump, the rescuer makes a forward leap downward with arms elevated forward or sideward just above shoulder height, shoulders ahead of hips, one leg extended forward with the other back (Fig. 60). Keeping the body at an angle on contact with the water will help keep the face above water and will keep the body moving forward. The legs come together underwater to stop possible sinking action, while the arms press down against the water. Subsequent stroking of arms and legs serves as a secondary effort to keep the head above water and to continue moving forward. The stride jump is used to enter deep water from a height of no more than 3 feet.

FIG. 60

Run-and-Plunge Dive

At a point at which running through deepening water becomes slower, the rescuer takes a shallow forward dive, keeping the head above water and the eyes on the victim.

Long, Shallow Dive

Where water and bottom conditions are known and the depth is at least 3 feet, a long, shallow dive is the fastest method of entering the water (Fig. 61). Since the head and eyes are submerged only momentarily and the rescuer is stroking forward almost immediately, this method of entry is most generally used.

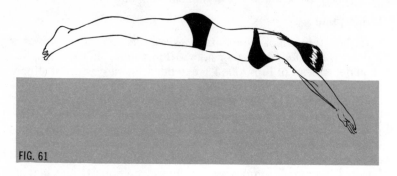

FIG. 61

Entering From a Height

For entering the water from heights greater than 3 feet, the rescuer should use a method of entry that is most suitable for existing water conditions and for the rescuer's skill. The rescuer may dive and thereby reach the victim faster, but in case of any doubt about diving, the entry should be a feet-first jump. The rescuer steps off with head erect but eyes on the victim (Fig. 62). After the rescuer makes contact with the water, the arms and legs may be spread to stop the descent and kept ready to propel the body back to the surface. For heights above 10 feet, it is preferable and safer for the rescuer to jump rather than to make a diving entry.

Approach Stroking

Since the rescuer should keep eyes fixed on the victim or on the spot where the victim was last seen, and since the victim should be reached as quickly as possible, the rescuer should employ the most effective swimming stroke with the modification of keeping the head high enough for visual contact with the victim. The crawl (Fig. 63) or the breast stroke (Fig. 64) is the approach stroke most commonly used.

However, the rescuer should not swim "all out," since enough energy must be conserved for towing the victim to safety.

FIG. 62

FIG. 63

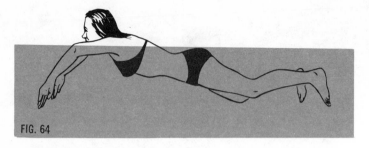

FIG. 64

Principles of Making Contact

The method of contacting the victim is based on fixed principles of making a safe rescue. The rescuer should never contact a victim until all possibilities for a noncontact rescue have been exhausted.

The rescuer must be in a ready and reversed position to seize the victim without being caught himself. The rescuer must be prepared to turn the victim around if necessary.

As soon as possible, the rescuer should bring the victim's face above water and keep it above the surface to facilitate the victim's breathing. This action will result, in most cases, in calming the victim, developing confidence in the rescuer, and insuring the victim's cooperation.

If the victim is thrashing, the rescuer should postpone making contact until the victim becomes passive and easily handled. The rescuer should talk to a conscious victim before making contact, saying, "Take it easy, I am going to help you."

Rescuers should always be prepared to evade a victim's grasp and to defend themselves. Active victims will usually be vertical in the water, with head back and arms extended forward and upward and thrashing against the water. Victims seldom do much kicking with their legs.

Swimming up to the victim, the rescuer must be in a ready position to avoid the victim's grasp. The rescuer must gain control so as to level off the victim from the vertical to the horizontal position and finally to get underway toward safety as soon as possible.

Since each rescue occurs under different conditions, the rescuer must use judgment and quickly decide which of the approaches, assists, and carries can best result in a safe rescue.

Reverse or Ready Position

If the victim is still at the surface, the rescuer approaches to a point just beyond the victim's reach and reverses body position.

FIG. 65

FIG. 66

Depending on the approach stroke being employed, the rescuer checks forward progress by sweeping one or both arms forward, coincident with tucking the legs forward (Fig. 65). The rescuer's legs are then forward of the chest and separated in order to be ready to kick while the arms are sculling (Fig. 66).

Facing the victim and just out of reach, the rescuer talks to the victim and attempts to calm him. The rescuer is also positioned to make contact or to avoid the victim's grasp.

If the victim's head sinks beneath the surface or the victim suddenly becomes passive, the rescuer may elect not to go into the reverse position but to make contact immediately.

Lifesaving Stroke

The lifesaving stroke is a fairly simple adaptation of the sidestroke. In towing or assisting a victim, the rescuer should use top arm for contact and support; hence, the stroke will consist of a pull of the lower arm timed with the scissors kick.

Lifesaving Stroke With Regular Scissors Kick

The top arm is held in an extended position over the side of the upper thigh, with the hand suspended just at the surface. The action of the lower arm, called the shallow arm pull, is basically the same as performed in the sidestroke.

The lower arm and the legs recover at the same time. The top leg will recover forward and the under leg back. The pull and kick will then be made simultaneously (Fig. 67), and there should be a

FIG. 67

minimal interval between each propulsive effort. Exhalation occurs during the pull of the arms and inhalation at the beginning of the recovery.

Lifesaving Stroke With Inverted Scissors Kick

The movement and timing used in this stroke are identical to those explained for the regular scissors except that the body is turned over to the opposite side. The top leg will be recovered back, while the under leg will be recovered forward (Fig. 68).

FIG. 68

Helping the Tired Swimmer

As the names indicate, the following assists are used in helping a swimmer who has become tired but is not in immediate danger of drowning. Such a situation often arises when two persons may be swimming side by side and one overestimates his ability and is having difficulty in continuing. The other swimmer can help by providing added support and encouragement and by assisting the tired swimmer to safety in the easiest way possible.

Arm Assist on Front

A novice or a tired swimmer who is swimming on the front can be aided by the rescuer's grasping him under the armpit, keeping the thumb up (Fig. 69). The rescuer thus can help support the swimmer and encourage the person to continue easy swimming movements. The rescuer can then make forward progress by using the lifesaving stroke or a modified breaststroke.

FIG. 69

Arm Assist on Back

A novice or tired swimmer who is swimming on the back or who can be assisted to the supine position can be grasped under the armpit (Fig. 70). From the reversed position, the rescuer supports the swimmer and encourages the person to relax and to continue easy swimming movements. Then the rescuer, maintaining contact at the armpit, makes forward progress using a modified breaststroke or the lifesaving stroke.

Arm Assist by Two Rescuers

When assisting the novice or tired swimmer who may be either on the front or back, a second rescuer may provide valuable assistance

FIG. 70

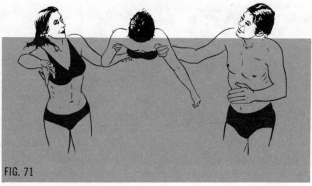

FIG. 71

by grasping the victim's other armpit (Fig. 71). The second rescuer thus gives additional support and propulsion. However, the second person should follow directions from the initial rescuer.

Tired-Swimmer Assist

If the rescuer determines that a tired swimmer may need more support than is provided by the armpit-assist techniques or because of the distance to safety, the following method may be used. The rescuer reverses position, talks with the victim, and calms him. When the rescuer is satisfied that the victim can and will follow directions, the rescuer swims in, maintaining some forward movement.

The rescuer, facing the tired swimmer, tells the swimmer to place hands on the rescuer's shoulders, keep the elbows straight, lay head and shoulders back on the water, and then separate the legs (Fig. 72). During this contact, the rescuer maintains forward motion by executing short and rapid breaststroke arm and leg movements. The tired swimmer should then be in a supine resting position, making it easier for the rescuer to push the victim along in front. The victim may be instructed to look the rescuer in the face for added confidence. Meanwhile, the rescuer should encourage the victim by talking calmly.

A gradual turn or change of direction is easily accomplished by the rescuer's maintaining propulsion throughout the maneuver. The rescuer places one hand on the side of one of the victim's arms, and this hand serves to maintain contact during the turn and to aid in pushing the victim around. The other arm strokes toward the victim's shoulder.

If the tired swimmer becomes panicky and seizes the rescuer around the head and shoulders and wraps the legs around the rescuer's body, the rescuer should make no effort to release himself but should simply lower the chin and keep on swimming. Since the victim at that point would be almost beneath the surface and would have little downward pull because of buoyancy, the resulting balanced position should enable the rescuer to continue stroking to gain shore or safety. If the distance to safety is great and the victim continually tries to climb upon the rescuer's head and shoulders, making it impractical to continue, the rescuer should submerge, use a front headhold release, and then attempt an appropriate carry.

FIG. 72

APPROACHES

Trained rescuers should be capable of handling a wide variety of emergency situations. However, rescuers should realize their own limitations in regard to skill and endurance so that they can avoid getting involved in attempting rescues that are beyond their capabilities. A rescuer should always use some extension, support, or rescue equipment when available.

On-the-spot judgment is necessary, since if a person appears to be in danger of disappearing beneath the surface, the victim should be contacted as soon as possible. If the victim is only a short distance away, swimming may be the quickest method of reaching and saving the person.

Approaching a victim from the rear is the safest method. However, there may be occasions when a front approach can be safely used if the victim's eyes are underwater. On some occasions, the would-be rescuer may simply kick and swim away from the victim's grasp while deciding on a safer approach.

If the struggling victim's head is above the surface and there is adequate water visibility, the rescuer may elect to use a front underwater approach. In most cases, the rescuer will find that a conscious victim will cooperate and follow simple directions as long as enough support is provided for adequate breathing. The need for quickly bringing and keeping a victim's mouth and nose above the surface is obvious.

Rear Approach—Armpit Level-Off

When a victim can be approached from behind, the rescuer swims to a point directly behind the victim and close to the victim's back. The rescuer reverses position from the horizontal to a position where the legs are well forward of the chest. The body twists while the rescuer separates the legs—top leg back and bottom leg forward. The legs are ready to deliver a series of short, vigorous leg strokes while making contact, keeping the victim's face above water and starting the victim moving.

The rescuer makes contact by reaching out with the forward arm and grasping the victim's armpit with the thumb in the up position (Fig. 73).

Immediately following contact, the rescuer can talk to the victim, instructing the person to "relax and place your head back." Generally, if the victim's face is free of the water, the victim will cooperate, thereby making it easier for the rescuer.

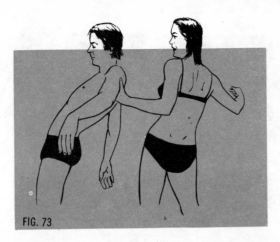

FIG. 73

Depending on the distance to safety, the cooperation of the victim, and the size and buoyancy of the victim, the rescuer may elect to continue towing by the armpit or may change to a tow that gives more control.

Rear Approach—Chin Level-Off

In this alternate contact method, the rescuer approaches, reverses, and positions himself just behind the victim. The rescuer makes contact by extending the forward arm across the victim's shoulder, close to the neck. The rescuer cups the victim's chin firmly in the palm of the hand while being careful not to apply pressure to the throat. To assist in leveling off and getting underway, the rescuer bends the elbow to pull the victim's head back, while using the victim's shoulder for leverage (Fig. 74). For better control, the rescuer may hold the victim's head tightly against the rescuer's shoulder. From the moment of contact, vigorous stroking with the rescuer's legs and the free arm will be necessary to change the victim from the vertical position to a moving horizontal position. The victim can then be placed into a carry for better control.

Rear Approach With Two-Hand Level-Off

Approaching from the rear, a rescuer may be faced with a situation in which there is difficulty in leveling off a victim who may be nonbuoyant and heavy in the water. To level off, the rescuer

FIG. 74

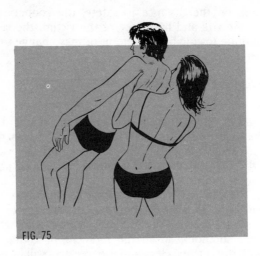

FIG. 75

submerges, grasps both of the victim's armpits, leans the body back, and applies leverage with both arms (Fig. 75). For this procedure to be effective, the rescuer must be kicking vigorously throughout. Once leveling and getting underway have been established, the rescuer may continue towing the victim with the armpit tow, using a vigorous lifesaving stroke.

Front Surface Approach

If the rescuer nears the victim and finds that the victim's head has sunk beneath the surface, no time should be lost in making contact and bringing the victim to the surface. When the rescuer is within arm's reach of the victim, the rescuer reverses position, exactly as in the rear approach. Timing his movement, the rescuer crosses down from above and seizes the back of the victim's wrist, with right hand to right wrist or left hand to left wrist. If the rescuer misses his grasp, making a quick leg kick and sculling with the arms in the water will drive him back and enable him to gauge when to make another grab. When a firm grasp is secured, the rescuer leans backward, pulls the victim's arm across the rescuer's body, twisting the wrist in line with the pull and alongside the rescuer's ear (Fig. 76A). To aid the rescuer in turning the victim and getting

FIG. 76A

FIG. 76B

underway, quick, vigorous leg kicks are essential. As soon as the victim's back is fully turned to the rescuer, the victim's armpit (Fig. 76B) or chin can be grasped, using the free hand. The wrist is then released. The rescuer then makes the choice of continuing with the armpit tow or changing to a control carry.

Underwater Approach

.When a victim's face is above the surface and the water is clear, the rescuer can make a quick vertical surface dive no closer than 6 feet in front of the victim (Fig. 77A). The dive should bring the rescuer down below the victim's feet, where the rescuer levels off and comes up to a point where the eyes are on a level with the victim's knees (Fig. 77B). The rescuer should then be vertical, with legs under him, prior to making contact. The rescuer places one hand in front of the victim's legs and the other in back, just above each knee, and turns the victim quickly so that the victim's back is

FIG. 77A

FIG. 77B

FIG. 77C

toward the rescuer. The rescuer's hands remain in contact with the victim's sides as the rescuer returns to the surface, constantly supporting the victim's body so that the victim's face is above water but without lifting the victim. Before the rescuer's head emerges, the rescuer grabs one of the victim's armpits (Fig. 77C) or chin to level off and get underway.

Approaching by Diving to Rear of Victim

When a victim is floundering about 20 feet or less from the side of a pool or pier, and speed in getting to the person is necessary, the rescuer may elect to perform a variation of a rear approach. Taking advantage of the momentum from the dive, the rescuer dives in and swims underwater, if necessary, and surfaces behind the victim (Fig. 78). From this position, the rescuer can proceed as in a regular rear approach.

FIG. 78

CARRIES (TOWS)

In attempting to carry a victim from deep water to safety (edge of pool, float, boat, shallow water, etc.), the rescuer accepts the handicap of swimming not only for himself but also for the victim and, while carrying the victim, the rescuer sacrifices the use of one or both arms. Furthermore, maintaining contact and keeping the victim's face above water results in a relatively inefficient swimming position, with increased resistance. A swimming rescue is always a difficult and tiring experience.

It is, therefore, evident that the efficiency of individual performance is more important than absolute uniformity of method. Superiority of one method as opposed to another is pointless, since every rescue will be different. The rescuer must always use experience and judgment to select and adapt the rescue technique in relation to swimming ability, condition and endurance at the time, water conditions, the distance to safety, and the size and condition of the victim.

The rescuer should understand the main advantages and disadvantages of each carry and assist, knowing when and how to safely shift from one to another. The cross-chest carry has good control and support and is the best all-round carry. For long distances, however, it may prove tiring. The rescuer, therefore, may elect to change to the hair carry or to an assist, depending on the condition and cooperation of the victim. The hair carry is recommended for long distances but is limited to be used only for passive victims and only when the victim has sufficient hair for a firm grasp. The wrist tow also is limited to passive victims, since the control factor is missing. The shirt or collar tow obviously can only be used when a victim is wearing a shirt or jacket.

Cross-Chest Carry

The cross-chest carry is the most satisfactory carry for rescuer and victim alike, since it provides good support and reasonable control and gives the victim a sense of security. It can be applied after any of the contact positions and is employed most frequently for the average carrying distance. Because the victim is directly over the rescuer, a heavy victim may interfere with the leg kick. Therefore, for longer distances, it may be necessary to shift to another technique.

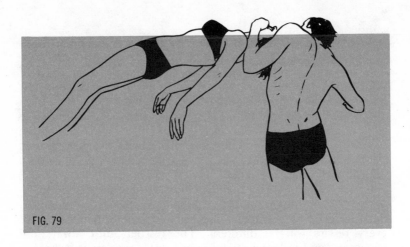

FIG. 79

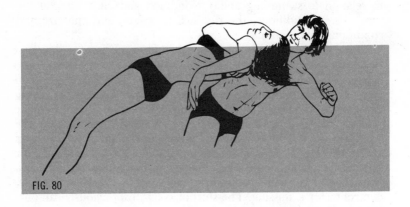

FIG. 80

After leveling off (Fig. 79) and getting underway, the rescuer brings the pulling arm over the corresponding shoulder of the victim, across the chest, until the rescuer's hand is in contact with the victim's side, just below the armpit (Fig. 80). The victim's shoulder should fit snugly into the rescuer's armpit, and the victim is held in a firm, snug grip against the rescuer's chest. This strong, steady hold will instill a sense of security in the victim. The rescuer will then be on the side, so that the hip will be directly beneath the small of the victim's back.

The rescuer will be using the lifesaving stroke, with either the regular scissor or the inverted scissor kick. The rescuer should check constantly to see that the victim's face is clear of the water, in addition to regularly turning the head to check direction.

Cross-Chest Control Position

For short distances and for temporary maximum control, the rescuer can grasp the wrist of the arm that is across the victim's chest (Fig. 81) and exert enough pull so that both hand and wrist are under the victim's armpit. This action will prevent the victim from twisting away from the rescuer's grasp.

The rescuer continues propulsion by using the strongest kick, whether it is the scissors, the inverted breaststroke kick, or a rotary kick.

FIG. 81

Hair Carry

The hair carry is relatively easy to learn and perform, since the extended arm holds the victim at a distance, and there is little interference with the rescuer's stroking. It is useful for long distances in smooth water, but the victim should be unconscious or semiconscious. The rescuer does not have good control and, in addition, this technique is not particularly comfortable or reassuring to a conscious victim. After leveling off using the chin or armpit method, the rescuer maintains contact and gets underway. The rescuer brings the stroking hand to the back of the victim's head, with fingers partially spread, and slides them through the hair up toward the forehead. The rescuer grasps as much of a handful of hair as possible. Depressing the wrist of the hand in contact with the hair, the rescuer straightens that arm, turns on the side and tows the victim (Fig. 82), checking constantly to keep the victim's face above the surface. To insure smooth and steady progress, the contact arm is kept straight but not rigid.

FIG. 82

Wrist Tow

This technique may be used to tow a passive victim for long distances and is a natural tow to use following the front surface approach. After the victim has been rolled over onto the back, the rescuer's towing arm is kept straight, and the pull must be made so that the victim's face remains above the surface. Adjusting the twist of the victim's wrist will change the victim's position to keep the face free.

If the rescuer has made initial contact with the hand at the victim's armpit or chin, the rescuer must first get the victim underway. Then, while kicking vigorously to keep forward movement, the rescuer uses the stroking arm to bring the victim's corresponding arm back. The rescuer can then grasp the victim's wrist, steadily straighten it behind the victim's head, and make steady progress with the wrist tow (Fig. 83).

If water conditions or the size and weight of the victim make this towing method difficult, or if the victim becomes too active, the rescuer should be prepared to move into a tow with better control.

FIG. 83

Shirt or Collar Tow

The shirt or collar tow method is similar to the hair carry except that the grip is made on the shirt or coat between the shoulder blades (Fig. 84). The grasp is made palm down, allowing some slack from the rescuer's hand up to the neck in order not to interfere with the victim's breathing. If the victim is passive, the towing arm provides some support for the head.

FIG. 84

REMOVAL OF VICTIM FROM WATER

The task of the rescuer is not ended until the victim has been removed or assisted from the water and transferred to a place of safety where first aid, medical attention, and rest may be available as required. Removal should be done as quickly as possible, however, with minimum risk of accident or further injury to the victim.

If the victim is not breathing, starting and continuing artificial respiration takes preference over removal of the victim.

In most cases, assistance will be available on shore, deck, or pier; therefore, the rescuer should use such help to facilitate continuation of artificial respiration during the removal or simply to make it easier for the tired rescuer and to minimize the risk of further injury to the victim. If there is any suspicion that the victim has incurred an injury to the neck or back, it is imperative for the person to be removed from the water only after having been placed and secured firmly on a backboard or other improvised rigid stretcher. Techniques for this removal are described in Chapter 12, "Emergency First Aid."

Shallow-Water Assist

When a tired swimmer or novice has been assisted to standing-depth water, he may be able to walk but needs some support. If the victim is on the rescuer's right side, the rescuer braces the victim with his right hand around the victim's waist. He then ducks his head under the victim's left arm (Fig. 85). He maintains a firm grasp on the victim's left arm, which is then across the rescuer's shoulder, and slowly helps the victim to walk to shore.

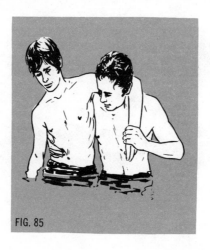

FIG. 85

Drag

Where there is a sloping beach, and especially when the victim is heavy, the safest and easiest method to use is the drag. The rescuer

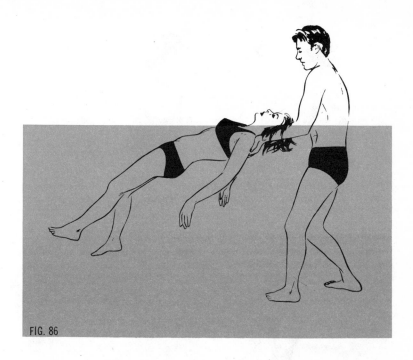

FIG. 86

gets behind the victim in standing-depth water and gets a good grasp up and under the victim's armpits. The victim's head is supported by the rescuer's forearms if necessary (Fig. 86). The rescuer walks slowly backward with the victim's body supported by the water. This method would make it possible for even a small rescuer to drag a heavy victim to a point where at least the victim's head and shoulders would be out of the water.

Team Lift

When help is available, the rescuer supports the victim in a supine position, approximately midway on the victim's trunk. One helper moves to a point opposite the rescuer, and both rescuers grasp hands under the victim's shoulders. Their other hands join at the small of the victim's back. The second helper supports the victim's legs (Fig. 87). Mouth-to-mouth resuscitation should be carried on during the removal if the victim is not breathing.

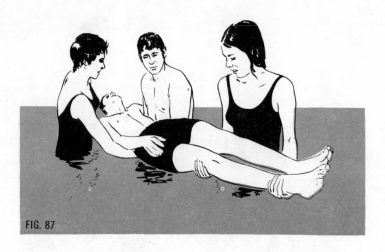

FIG. 87

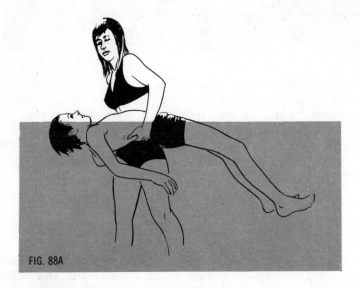

FIG. 88A

Saddle-Back Carry

In this method, the victim is carried just over the back of the hips, and the resulting weight distribution and low center of gravity enable a rescuer to carry a heavier victim without undue strain. The

FIG. 88B

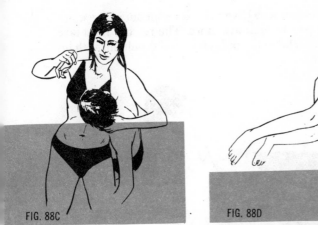

FIG. 88C

FIG. 88D

rescuer stands in waist-deep water and supports the victim's body in a horizontal position. Standing at the victim's side, facing the victim's head, the rescuer reaches across the victim's abdomen down to the far side of the body to support the victim with the hand (Fig. 88A). The rescuer then reaches over and across with his other hand, grasps the victim's wrist, and carries the arm upward until it rests across the rescuer's shoulders (Fig. 88B). He hangs on to the victim's wrist until the arm supporting the victim's body is slipped around the body close to the shoulders, where he takes a good hold

(Fig. 88C). The rescuer then turns his back to the victim, releases the wrist, and with his free hand reaches back to gather in both of the victim's legs at the knees. The victim's body is then tucked in and is across the rescuer's back, just above the hips (Fig. 88D). If necessary to keep the victim's face out of water, the hand supporting the shoulder can be slipped forward under the neck for support. The rescuer moves toward shore, and as the water gets shallower, he should move the hand at the victim's neck back to a position under the shoulder for ease of carrying.

On shore, to let the victim down, the rescuer carefully kneels on one knee, then on both knees, toes pointed backward, and sits back on his heels. After the legs and hips of the victim have touched the ground, the rescuer releases his grasp around the victim's legs and brings his free hand to support the head as the upper part of the body touches the ground.

When carrying, the rescuer should walk with trunk bent slightly forward to compensate for the victim's weight.

Lift From Water

Occasionally the rescuer may have to lift a victim out of the water onto a pool deck or pier without assistance. The rescuer must take great care not to injure the victim or himself and should lift with his legs instead of his back.

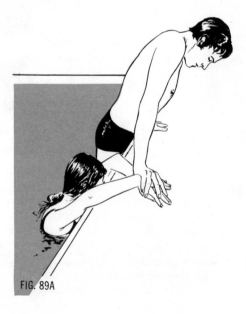

FIG. 89A

The rescuer tows the victim to the edge of the pool or pier, gets a good handhold on the edge, and turns the victim so that he faces the wall or pier. Supporting the victim so that his face remains above the surface, the rescuer places the victim's hands, one on top of the other, on the deck or pier. The rescuer places one hand on top of the victim's hands, moves to one side, and climbs or "breasts" himself out of the water (Fig. 89A). Maintaining contact, the rescuer pivots to face the victim and grasps the victim's wrists firmly. The rescuer should be standing as near the edge as possible. Dipping the victim's body once to gain some momentum, the rescuer lifts the body until the upper trunk clears the deck level (Fig. 89B). Stepping back, the rescuer lowers the victim's upper body to a prone position (Fig. 89C), being careful to protect the head. Securing the victim with one hand, the rescuer reaches with his free hand to the thigh and swings the legs onto the deck (Fig. 89D). If the rescuer cannot lift a heavy victim out of the water, he should support both himself and the victim by hanging onto the edge of the pool or pier while waiting for help.

FIG. 89B

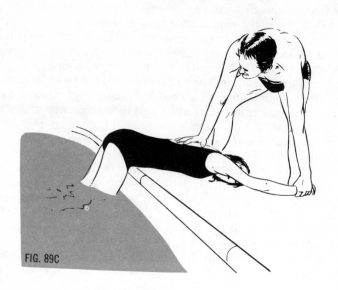

FIG. 89C

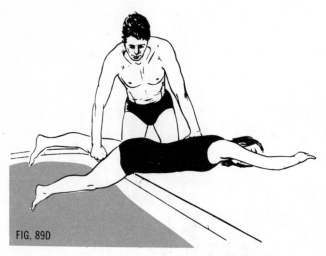

FIG. 89D

5

DEFENSES, RELEASES, AND ESCAPES

In an unusual situation such as the sudden capsizing of a craft, involving a number of persons, or when a rescuer is attempting to contact a victim, there is always the possibility that a victim may succeed in grasping the rescuer. This occurrence could be the result of the rescuer's misjudging distance, unfavorable water conditions, panic on the part of a tired swimmer, or poor visibility. Potential rescuers must be trained and prepared to meet such emergencies.

Since a drowning person usually seeks support in order to continue to get air, the struggling victim will, in most cases, end up by getting a hold about the rescuer's head or shoulders unless the rescuer prevents the victim from doing so. This upward struggle by the victim will have the result of pressing or forcing the rescuer under the surface. The natural impulse is to keep one's head above water. To do so, however, would mean supporting two persons, one of whom (the victim) is often better able to breathe than the potential rescuer. Instead a trained rescuer should take a quick breath of air, tuck in his chin, and deliberately pull both himself and the victim underwater. Commonly, the victim taken underwater releases his grip to reach the surface.

A potential rescuer should, therefore, be familiar with several methods for evading the victim, breaking contact, and releasing the victim's grasp. It must be understood that no one technique will be effective in all cases. Breath control, watermanship, and the ability to keep a cool head in a variety of situations can only be achieved by an understanding of the principles involved and by repeated practice in a variety of simulated situations.

PRACTICE FOR RELEASES AND ESCAPES

After practicing the skills on land and in chest-deep water and prior to practice in deep water, all lifesaving candidates should clearly understand that a signal such as the rescuer's pinching his partner is a "let go" signal. If anything goes wrong while practicing underwater, the rescuer cannot ask the practice partner to let go; therefore, an agreed-upon signal is vital for safety's sake.

In the initial practice session, the victim should apply holds firmly but with no thought in mind of making the practice release impossible. As skills are perfected, the victim can use surprise tricks or movements in an attempt to confound the rescuer. The victim can apply holds tightly, can shift arm and head positions unexpectedly, and, following one release, can quickly apply another hold. Being able to deal with such tactics will help to increase the confidence of a rescuer in his ability to meet actual conditions found in a drowning situation.

DEFENSES

The Block

When a rescuer is too close to make a proper approach, he extends the forward arm and places the hand with fingers spread against the upper part of the victim's chest (Fig. 90). Since the victim's reaction will be an attempt to grasp the rescuer's head and shoulders, the rescuer should quickly reverse and duck his head away from the victim's reaching arms.

FIG. 90

Block and Carry

In most cases, the victim will grab the rescuer's extended arm but should not be permitted to climb onto the rescuer's head and shoulders. If the distance to shore is not too great, the rescuer may turn on the side and swim to safety using the lifesaving stroke, with the victim hanging onto the extended arm (Fig. 91).

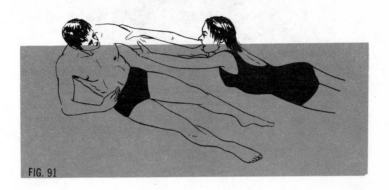

FIG. 91

If the victim has not been successful in grabbing the rescuer's arm, the rescuer has the option of either swimming out of reach before attempting another approach or immediately grasping one of the victim's wrists to start a front approach.

Block and Turn

If the distance to safety is more than 10 yards or if the length and strength of the victim's arms are causing difficulty, the rescuer may elect to turn the victim and go into a carry with better control. To accomplish this turn, the rescuer bends his blocking arm in order to attain better leverage for his free hand. The rescuer brings his free hand up from underneath, just above the victim's elbow, with the thumb inside of the arm (Fig. 92). The rescuer makes a simultaneous hand press against the victim's chest and a thrust up and across the rescuer's blocking arm. This action should release the victim's grasp and turn the victim. The rescuer quickly withdraws the blocking arm and uses this arm to level off the victim, gets underway, and goes into a carry.

FIG. 92

RELEASES AND ESCAPES

Double-Grip-on-One-Wrist Release

A potential rescuer, upon attempting a front approach, may ride the last stroke too far before reversing, thereby making it possible for the victim to grab the extended arm. To make the release, the rescuer uses the opposite arm and the leg on the side of that arm. The rescuer should immediately reverse position and reach across with his free hand to grasp the victim's far wrist from above and over the victim's extended arm. Taking a firm grip with the thumb on the outside, the rescuer presses down with his forearm on the victim's arms in order to submerge the victim. The rescuer stays at or close to the surface, since in that relative position he will be able to achieve greater leverage.

Without pause, the rescuer's foot (the foot on the same side as the arm that is pressing and grasping the victim's wrist) comes up over the victim's arm to the corresponding shoulder (Fig. 93A). The heel of the foot is placed close to the neck.

Holding the victim's wrist firmly, the rescuer presses by extending his leg down and away to break the victim's grasp (Fig. 93B).

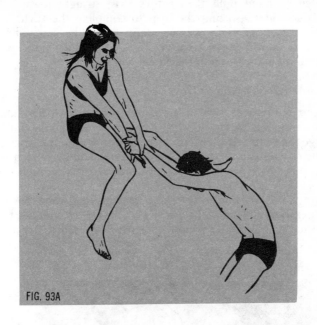

FIG. 93A

FIG. 93B

The rescuer's hand pulls the victim's wrist straight toward the rescuer's shoulder, twisting the arm to complete the turn. The rescuer's legs stroke vigorously for support, for leveling off and getting underway. The rescuer's free hand levels off at the victim's chin or armpit in preparation for the carry.

Escape From Double Grip on Wrist

Under circumstances where a rescuer decides that he should break contact and escape for his own safety, he should quickly submerge the victim. If the victim is still holding onto the rescuer's wrist, the rescuer can reach across with his free hand, grab his own fist, and pull quickly and firmly upward and toward himself (Fig. 94).

Stroking backward quickly with both arms and legs should enable the rescuer to escape out of the victim's reach. The rescuer can then decide what techniques can most effectively be used to assist the victim.

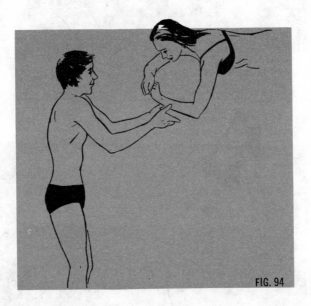

FIG. 94

Front-Head-Hold Release

When grasped around the head and shoulders from the front, the rescuer should immediately take a quick breath of air, tuck in his chin, and submerge both himself and the victim. Without pause,

FIG. 95A

FIG. 95B

the rescuer places his hands on the front of the victim's hips with
the heel of the hands against the body and the extended fingers
and thumbs grasping the victim's sides (Fig. 95A). By forcefully
pressing and extending his arms, the rescuer pushes the victim's

FIG. 95C

FIG. 95D

body back and up toward the horizontal position (Fig. 95B). The leverage thus applied will loosen the victim's grasp sufficiently, enabling the rescuer to free his head by tucking his chin inward and hunching his shoulders. The victim can then be quickly turned to a face-up position and should then be nearly horizontal (Fig. 95C).

Maintaining contact, the rescuer kicks vigorously, slides up behind the victim, levels off (Fig. 95D), and gets underway, using an effective carry.

Escape From Front Head Hold

When grasped in the front head hold, the rescuer may decide to break contact and escape in order to attempt an alternate technique. Immediately upon being grabbed, the rescuer takes a quick breath, tucks in his chin, and submerges with the victim. On the way down, the rescuer brings his hands up to the undersides of the victim's arms. By vigorously pushing straight upward, keeping his chin tucked and his shoulders hunched, the rescuer should be successful in getting free (Fig. 96). He then can quickly swim backward out of reach, surface, and decide on a safer approach.

FIG. 96

Rear-Head-Hold Release

Occasionally, a swimmer may be grasped from behind. However, such a predicament seldom results during an actual swimming rescue, since it is not conceivable that a rescuer would turn his back to a victim. It could result from a boat capsize or sudden panic on the part of a tired swimmer or novice. A panic-stricken person would grasp the nearest unsuspecting swimmer. This grasp is usually applied without warning.

As the rescuer feels that someone is attempting to grasp him, he should get a quick "bite" of air and tuck his chin down and to the side in order to protect his throat. The rescuer should then submerge, taking the victim with him. If the victim releases his grasp, the rescuer can quickly swim out of reach and make a safer, planned approach to rescue the victim.

To release the hold, the rescuer grasps the hand of the victim's lower arm, palm to palm, and, at the same time, the rescuer brings the other hand up vertically to grab the victim's lower arm at the elbow (Fig. 97A). By twisting inward and down on the victim's hand and pushing the victim's elbow upward, the rescuer releases the grip and places the victim's forearm straight across the victim's back (Fig. 97B). From this position behind the victim, the rescuer can use rotating pressure on the victim's arm behind the back to arch the victim upward and back (Fig. 97C). The rescuer's hand releases the victim's elbow, and the rescuer uses this hand to level off in preparation for a swimming carry.

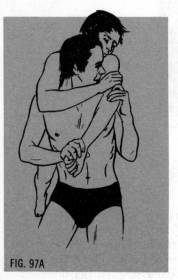

FIG. 97A

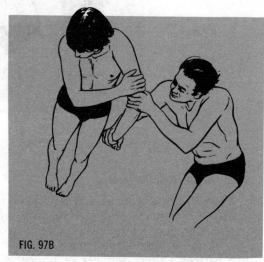

FIG. 97B

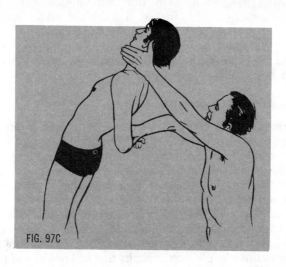

FIG. 97C

Escape From Rear Head Hold

To break contact and escape from the rear head hold, the rescuer must quickly tuck his chin down and to the side while taking a quick "bite" of air. After submerging both himself and the victim, the

FIG. 98

rescuer brings his hands up to the underside of each of the victim's elbows. By keeping his chin tucked in and his shoulders hunched, the rescuer pushes forcefully upward to free his head and push the victim back and away (Fig. 98). The rescuer should then swim well out of reach of the victim before surfacing and deciding what alternative rescue technique to use.

Double-Drowning Release

Quite frequently, a swimmer or novice untrained in lifesaving techniques, in attempting to rescue a victim, will be grasped by the victim. Two nonswimmers may suddenly step into deep water, panic, grab each other, and become locked in a struggle. Such cases lead to a struggle to stay at the surface, ending in the exhaustion of both, then submersion, and ultimate drowning.

When such an occurrence takes place a few feet from shore, the *trained* rescuer should make an initial, vigorous effort to tow both victims to safety. This effort can be attempted by swimming to the rear of the victim who got into difficulty first (if known) and using a hair carry or armpit tow (Fig. 99).

FIG. 99

If it is necessary to separate the two victims, the rescuer should get behind the first victim, should seize that victim by the chin with both hands, and, bearing down with the forearms, should submerge both victims (Fig. 100A). In submerging both victims, the rescuer rides his weight high and brings one foot over the locked arms and

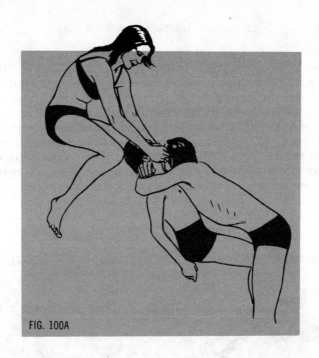

FIG. 100A

FIG. 100B

places that foot against the shoulder of the second victim, as close as possible to the victim's neck, with the heel inside (Fig. 100B). By pressing down and away (not kicking) and pulling up and back on the first victim's chin, the rescuer separates the two (Fig. 100C). Maintaining contact with one hand at the first victim's chin, the rescuer levels the victim off and gets underway for the carry. After carrying the first victim to safety, the rescuer may return to assist the other victim if resuscitation does not have to be applied to the first one. If another rescuer is available, the second rescuer should go to assist the other victim.

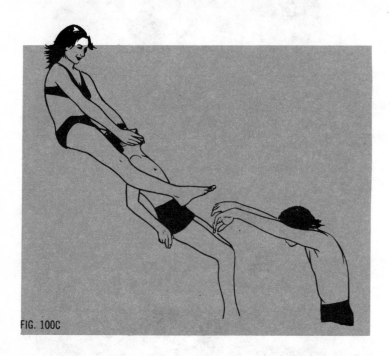

FIG. 100C

6

SEARCHING FOR AND RESCUING A SUBMERGED VICTIM

When a victim has disappeared beneath the surface, recovery must be made with utmost speed if the victim is to be successfully resuscitated. It is important for the location of the victim to be reasonably well established. Observations of untrained eyewitnesses of drowning accidents are usually unreliable because the excitement induced by the accident usually prevents accurate estimation of time, location, and circumstances surrounding the drowning.

Use of scuba equipment is the preferred method of underwater search and recovery. However, it is seldom that trained scuba divers are readily available to rescue a submerged victim in time to resuscitate the person. It is therefore necessary for swimmers and lifesavers to be able to use less effective but quicker means of searching for and recovering a victim.

Depth of water, clarity, temperature, and waves or current are all factors that must be considered in search and rescue. In addition, available help, plus search and rescue equipment, will determine the most feasible procedures.

RECOVERY OF SUBMERGED VICTIM FROM SHORE

To rescue a submerged victim in deep water, a potential rescuer who lacks swimming skill must confine the rescue efforts to using available equipment. If the victim can be seen lying on the bottom, as in the case of drowning off a pier, a shepherd's crook (see page 30) or a boathook offers the only practical means for a non-swimmer to bring the submerged person to the surface. The boathook is a piece of boating equipment commonly found on small craft and around docks and marinas. It consists of a hook and a pike attached to a long pole. With such a device, the victim's clothing or swimsuit may be caught, and the victim can then be pulled to the surface.

The shepherd's crook is a piece of rescue equipment designed especially for use in swimming pools. Many states require that such a device be readily available at all pools. With it, the victim's body may be encircled and drawn to the surface.

In murky or dark water where the victim cannot be seen, the nonswimmer can help by watching the spot where the victim went down and can then help a swimmer who comes to the rescue by pointing out where the victim was last seen.

RECOVERY OF VICTIM BY SURFACE DIVING

If the victim goes down as the rescuer is swimming toward him, no time should be lost in recovering him. With eyes fixed on the spot where the victim was last seen, the rescuer continues his

FIG. 101

FIG. 102

approach and, upon reaching that spot, does a surface dive (Fig. 101). Upon locating the victim, the rescuer grasps the victim's chin, hair, or armpit from behind (Fig. 102), plants his feet on the bottom, if it is firm, and pushes off from the bottom and strokes and kicks his way to the surface. If the bottom is soft and muddy, the rescuer must depend entirely on arm and leg strokes to pull the victim to the surface.

When there is doubt as to the location of the victim, the trained lifesaver must survey the situation and plan a course of action. First, the rescuer must determine the general area in which the victim is supposed to have submerged. He can look for telltale bubbles rising to the surface. If there are none and the water is clear, the rescuer should systematically swim across the area with his face in the water and scan the bottom. If the bottom is dark, light clothing, a swimming suit, or the gleam of bare arms and legs can often be detected.

On white sand, dark clothing and dark color of hair can indicate the location of the victim. If the victim is located, the rescuer does a surface dive, swims to a. position behind the victim, grasps the victim by chin, hair, or armpit, and swims him to the surface.

In murky or dark water of a depth that can be reached by surface diving, the rescuer can search the area by using a series of systematic surface dives. The rescuer surface dives, either headfirst or feetfirst, and attempts to cover the designated area of the bottom in a series of overlapping lanes until the victim is found or until the rescuer is satisfied that the victim is not in that section. After each dive, the rescuer swims along the bottom for two or three body lengths and then surfaces. He should move back about 3 feet and then repeat the process. Attempting to swim along the bottom for a considerable distance can quickly exhaust the rescuer, and if he is not lucky in finding the victim on the first few attempts, he may be unable to continue long enough to cover a designated area in the search. Using a systematic formation or pattern whereby every square foot of the bottom can be examined is always preferable, whether the searching is done by a single rescuer or a group of swimmers.

GROUP SEARCH OF BOTTOM

A group of rescuers can, of course, cover an area of bottom more quickly and effectively than one or two people, but they must work together under the firm direction of a leader who gives the signals and directions.

Rescuers line up in a straight line, no more than an arm's length apart. At the leader's signal, they surface dive to within 1 foot of the bottom. They then swim along the bottom and swim easily for a preestablished number of strokes. They then come straight up to the surface. The swimmers back up about 3 feet and again, following the leader's directions, repeat the process and continue the search (Fig. 103).

Failure to move back before making the next dive may mean that an area just beyond the previous surface dive has been missed.

USE OF MASK, FINS, AND SNORKEL IN SEARCH AND RESCUE

Where face mask, fins, and snorkel are available for single or group rescue, visibility is increased, as is the ability to cover larger

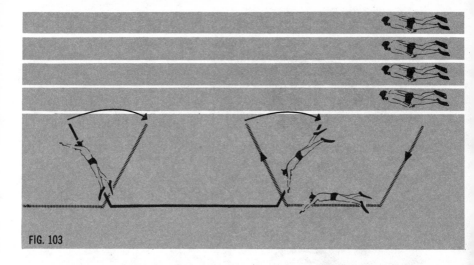

FIG. 103

areas more quickly and effectively. Use of this equipment for rescue purposes requires familiarity and training in proper usage; therefore its selection and use are included in lifesaving training courses.

Equipment Information

Basic equipment used for underwater search and recovery consists of a mask, fins, and a snorkel. The most important item is the mask, which provides visibility for the swimmer when swimming on the surface with the face in the water or when swimming underwater. The fins provide propulsion that enables the swimmer to cover large search areas quickly and with little effort. The snorkel allows the swimmer to breathe as he swims on the surface with face in the water and is of great value when used with the mask to scan the bottom rapidly.

Mask

Masks should be constructed of soft, flexible rubber with an untinted, shatterproof safety glass facepiece, held in position by a corrosion-proof metal band (Fig. 104A). A single or a divided strap holds the mask in place and can be adjusted to fit the diver's head.

Some masks are equipped with a purge valve, which allows the individual to clear water from the mask by exhaling through the nose (Fig. 104B). Masks with a nose-blocking device, or with a molded indentation to fit the nose, enable the swimmer to block off

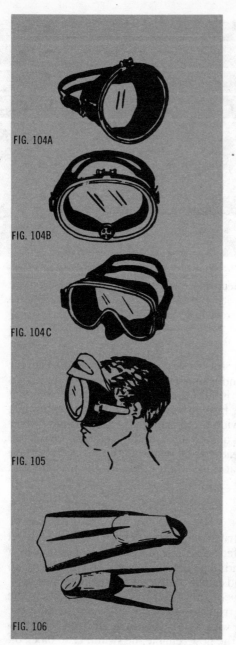

FIG. 104A

FIG. 104B

FIG. 104C

FIG. 105

FIG. 106

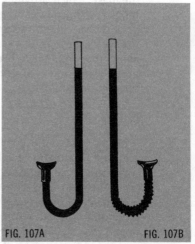

FIG. 107A   FIG. 107B

or pinch the nose to equalize air pressure in the ear canal as the person dives more deeply (Fig. 104C).

To test for proper fit, the swimmer places the mask against the face without applying the head strap. If the mask is properly sealed, when the swimmer inhales through the nose, the mask will stay in place without being held (Fig. 105).

Fins

Fins are constructed in various ways. Some float; others do not. Some are designed with a full foot and are worn like a shoe; others are open at the heel and are held in position by a heel strap (Fig. 106).

Fins should be selected so that they fit the feet properly to avoid chafing or cramping during use and should have the proper flexibility and blade size for the strength of the swimmer's kick.

Snorkel

Snorkels used by skilled swimmers are J-shaped rubber tubes from 12 to 15 inches in length. Some are molded in one piece (Fig. 107A), while others have a ribbed, flexible section for the curved portion of the tube (Fig. 107B). All are fitted with a soft rubber, flanged mouthpiece, which should be the right size for the user so that water cannot seep in as the person breathes.

Skill Practice

Mask

- Defogging faceplate
  To prevent the faceplate's fogging while being used underwater, before putting it on, rub the inside of the glass with saliva, leaves, kelp, or glycerine and then rinse it off with water.
- Putting on mask
  Place mask over your face first and then pull the strap over your head. This procedure prevents getting hair between mask and face.
- Checking for leaks and defogging effectiveness
  With mask in place, submerge until your head is below the surface. If the mask leaks, come to the surface and adjust the strap. Repeat the defogging procedure if the glass continues to fog over.
- Flooding and emptying mask
  Submerge and flood mask by lifting an edge. Surface and empty mask by raising the lower edge from your face. Submerge and

flood mask again. While in a horizontal swimming position, turn your head to one side to pocket the water on the lower side. Press top side of mask firmly to your face and exhale forcefully through your nose, forcing the water out under the lower side of mask.

- Relieving mask pressure
  With mask in position, submerge and exhale a little air through your nose to show how mask face pressure, caused by water pressure, can be relieved as the depth of the dive increases.
- Relieving ear pressure
  Ear pressure also increases as the diver goes deeper, and may cause some pain. This pressure may be relieved by pressing the mask against your face and exhaling through your nose, or by swallowing and moving your jaws. Masks equipped with a nose-blocking device or a molded nose indentation simplify the process of equalizing pressure.

Fins

- Walking with fins
  The swimmer should wet both the fins and feet before putting the fins on. Wetting makes it easier to pull the fins over the feet. While wearing fins, the person should always walk backward either on land or in shallow water to avoid tripping.
- Kicking while wearing fins
  While wearing fins, the swimmer uses a crawl kick. However, the kicking action is slower and deeper, with a greater knee bend. While swimming at or near the surface, the swimmer should keep the fins in the water, since letting the fins come out of the water during the kicking action will greatly lessen the effectiveness of kicking with fins.

Snorkel

- Securing snorkel
  The snorkel is secured by placing it between the mask strap and your head or by slipping the snorkel through the snorkel keeper. Use of the snorkel keeper is recommended, since its use will keep the mask and snorkel secure and the snorkel at the proper angle.
- Holding mouthpiece
  The mouthpiece should be inserted in the mouth with the flange placed between the lips and teeth and gripped with the teeth.
- Snorkel breathing
  With a snorkel in place, the swimmer can then inhale and exhale through the snorkel (Fig. 108). Initially, the swimmer should

FIG. 108

practice breathing by submerging the face while starting in chest-deep water. After the swimmer can comfortably breathe while standing, snorkel breathing can be practiced while swimming at the surface with the face in the water.

• Flooding and emptying snorkel
Initially, practice in flooding and emptying the snorkel should be practiced in standing-depth water, before attempting this skill while surface diving and surfacing in deeper water. The swimmer takes a breath, submerges, and floods the snorkel. the swimmer returns to the surface, keeps the face surmerged, and expels the water from the snorkel by *forceful* mouth exhalation through the tube. The swimmer should then breathe in carefully in the event that some water remains in the curve of the snorkel. If some water remains, the swimmer should again exhale to force out the rest of the water before continuing to breathe through the snorkel.

Swimming Practice

• Swimming on the surface
The normal swimming position when wearing mask, fins, and snorkel is with the arms at the side and face in the water (Fig. 109). Since the swimmer can breathe through the snorkel and does not have to lift the face to breathe, scanning the bottom when searching for a submerged victim or object is more efficient.

• Surface diving and surfacing
The swimmer performs a surface dive by rolling forward into a tuck or pike position (Fig. 110). On returning to the surface, the diver should stop, look up, listen, and extend the hands overhead

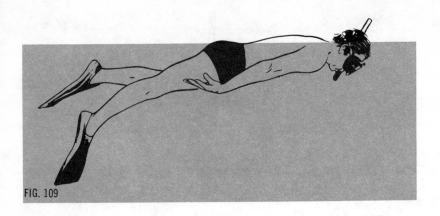

FIG. 109

FIG. 110

before surfacing (Fig. 111). This action is a safety precaution and should be standard procedure to follow when surfacing after each dive.

- Swimming underwater

  Swimming underwater while wearing fins can best be accomplished by using the leg action only. The arms can be carried forward for protection when swimming in unclear water, for more efficient searching for submerged object or victim, or for avoiding obstacles found on the bottom (Fig. 112).

FIG. 111

FIG. 112

- Entering the water
  Starting from deck or pool edge, the swimmer holds the mask
  securely to his face and steps off in the stride position. From low
  elevation or from the gunwale of a small boat, the swimmer can
  roll in, holding the mask securely, keeping chin down, hitting the
  water on the back of the neck and shoulders (Fig. 113). Swimmers
  should not attempt to dive into the water head foremost.

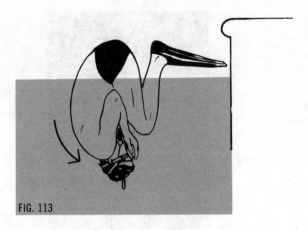

FIG. 113

UNDERWATER SEARCH AND RECOVERY BY GRAPPLING

Underwater search and recovery of water accident victims can, under certain conditions, such as deep or extremely cold water, be carried out from the surface or from the shore by using grappling gear.

There is a remote possibility that grappling equipment could be put into operation in time to save the life of a submerged victim of a water accident, but, generally speaking, because of the time it may take to assemble the necessary gear and personnel, the problem usually becomes one of recovery rather than rescue.

In grappling, a plan of operation or a search pattern that will provide for a thorough coverage of the accident area is essential. When a water accident occurs near anchored or permanently located objects, such objects provide a base from which the search can be initiated (Fig. 114). When present, currents must be taken into account if a low specific gravity of the lost object prevents it from sinking rapidly to the bottom. The presence of air bubbles may help pinpoint the location of the lost object. It is sometimes possible for an observer to get a fix on an accident that happens a considerable distance from shore. A fix can be obtained by lining up the accident site with two stationary objects on the opposite shore from two observation points a few hundred feet apart. Using long

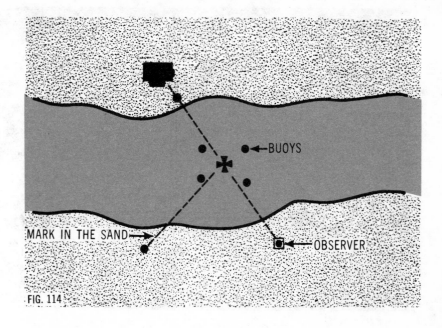

FIG. 114

poles, oars, or marks in the sand pointing to the accident scene from two different locations is an alternate method of establishing a fix.

After arrival at the accident scene, search craft should mark the area with buoys. A check of the buoys will also indicate whether currents are present.

The search pattern and the choice of grappling gear are determined by the shape, size, and consistency of the lost object, the depth and nature of the bottom, and other conditions, such as water currents and weather. Three types of gear—grappling irons, a grappling pole, and a grappling line—are generally used in recovery work.

Grappling Irons

Grappling irons are standard equipment at most water recreation areas and with rescue squads. They can be rigged either with sharp, barbless hooks or with a large, malleable metal gang hook arrangement designed for snagging objects that have angular or impenetrable surfaces (Fig. 115). The pliable hook will straighten out under heavy tension, thus preventing the gear from fouling. The sharp gang hooks do not bend easily and should, therefore, be

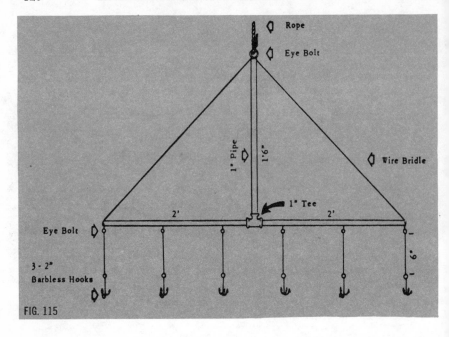

Rope

Eye Bolt

1" Pipe

1'6"

Wire Bridle

1" Tee

2'

2'

Eye Bolt

3 - 2"
Barbless Hooks

6'

FIG. 115

secured to the rig with a 60-pound test fishline that can be broken when the rig is fouled.

Grappling irons are usually towed behind a slowly moving outboard boat or rowboat (Fig. 116). If outboards without remote controls are used, it may be advisable to operate them stern-first, with the lineman in the bow (Fig. 117). The line should be held in the hands and should extend behind the boat at an angle of 45 degrees.

Start the search pattern with a sweep over the center of the marked-off or suspected area (Fig. 118). When the object is hooked, stop the boat and allow it to drift back over the object as the grappling line is slowly taken in.

Raise the irons slowly to the surface and remove the object or clear the hooks of any accumulated trash. A line should be attached and the hooks should be removed from a heavy object while it is waterborne. Lower the irons directly over the spot from which they were raised if the search has to be continued.

Grappling irons can be rigged with two lines and operated between two lines and between two points (Fig. 119). Narrow streams and ponds can be covered quickly by using this technique.

FIG. 116

45°

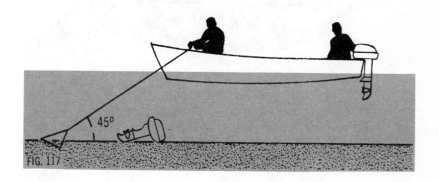

45°

FIG. 117

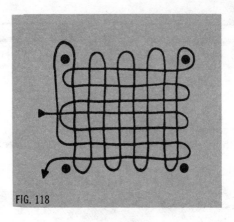

FIG. 118

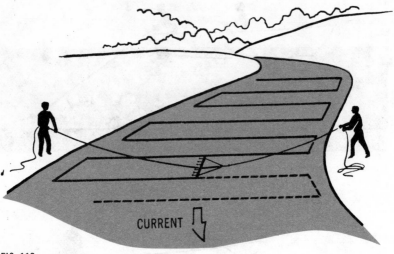

FIG. 119

Grappling Pole

A 12- to 16-foot grappling pole with a large single or a gang barbless hook firmly attached to one end is excellent for probing in rocky, grassy, or other areas where underwater debris precludes dragging operations (Fig. 120).

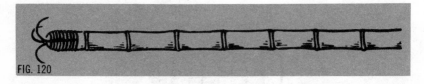

FIG. 120

Grappling Line

A weighted grappling line can be used to recover victims from narrow, deep channels or from defiles between rocks. Large, three-pointed gang hooks can be worked in between the three strands of a

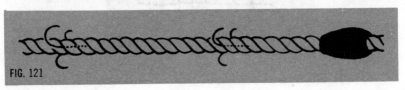

FIG. 121

⅜-inch manila line of suitable length (Fig. 121). The hooks protrude between each of the three strands, and the shank can be worked down between the strands into the core of the line. A few turns with a strong piece of twine around the line and over the shank will firmly hold the hook in position. Ten to twelve ounces of lead in front of the hooks will keep the line on the bottom as it is pulled or towed.

A 75- or 100-foot weighted line, with gang hooks spaced 4 or 5 feet apart and placed back to back, can be used to sweep a shallow offshore area along a beachfront (Fig. 122). Hold or anchor one end of the line and wade in or use a boat to swing the free end out and around in a half circle. The free end is then held or anchored, and the other end is brought around in another half circle. The maneuver is repeated as often as necessary.

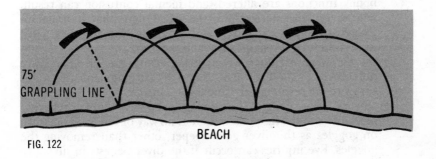

75'
GRAPPLING LINE

BEACH

FIG. 122

RELATED SAFETY INFORMATION
FOR THE SPORT OF SKIN DIVING

The information in this chapter on the use of mask, fins, and snorkel should not be considered as sufficient training to equip the lifesaver to be qualified in this sport. The following suggestions are presented as introductory information only.

• Before doing any diving, have a physical examination and get the doctor's approval to dive.
• Enroll in a complete course of instruction before diving in open-water areas.
• Always swim and dive with a buddy, never alone, and know where your buddy is at all times.
• Divers should be skilled swimmers and lifesavers. Minimum skills include being able to tread water, float, scull, surface dive, swim

underwater, swim 440 yards using a stroke on the front and on the back, and perform a swimming rescue.

- In the early stages of learning, you should not dive deeper than 10 feet. It must be remembered that pressure increases rather rapidly as a diver descends. A broad guide of 1 pound of pressure per square inch for each 2 feet of descent emphasizes this pressure increase. A depth of 16 feet would, therefore, equal 8 pounds. This pressure added to the normal atmospheric pressure of 14.7 pounds totals 22.7 pounds of pressure on each square inch of the diver's body. It is this pressure that causes mask squeeze and ear pain.
- Hyperventilation, or deep breathing to prolong the diver's ability to stay underwater longer, should be discouraged. Hyperventilation increases the oxygen intake but lowers the carbon dioxide in the bloodstream. When the carbon dioxide content is lowered, bodily functions are altered, and mental confusion can result. The diver fails to recognize the usual signs that indicate his oxygen supply is exhausted and may lose consciousness while underwater. Unless help is available, he drowns.
- Do not wear earplugs when diving. During a dive, pressure differences in the ear canal caused by earplugs and the water pressure can result in permanent ear damage.
- Do not wear goggles for diving purposes. Unlike relieving pressure with the face mask, there is no way of relieving pressure on goggles as the diver goes deeper, other than removing the goggles. Eye injuries can occur if the diver persists in diving to depths wearing goggles.
- An important safety practice when diving in open-water areas is to have a boat or some type of float close at hand. A boat is preferred. When a boat is not available, an improvised float can be made from a good innertube and a clothes basket or net material, to provide a resting support for the diver and a receptacle in which to store articles (Fig. 123). Boats or floats should be equipped with the proper anchor and a line long enough and strong enough to anchor them securely during high wind or wave action.
- The inflatable vest is a valuable item for the safety of the skin diver and should be worn at all times when diving in open-water areas. The vest should be designed to inflate by cartridge, and by mouth for emergencies, and should support the diver's head with the face out of water (Fig. 124). This support is very important in the event the diver loses consciousness.
- The diver's flag, which may be purchased or constructed, is a reddish-orange rectangle with a diagonal white stripe (Fig. 125).

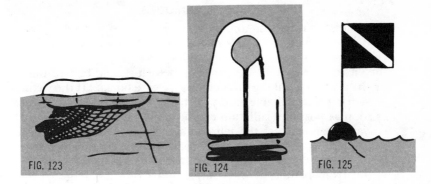

FIG. 123   FIG. 124   FIG. 125

It is flown from the diver's boat or float to warn craft in the area that a diver is below or in the vicinity. When displayed, the flag should be at least 3 feet above the surface to provide good visibility. Swimming and diving activities should be confined to within 100 feet of the flag.

- The unskilled diver should avoid surging seas, swift currents, and murky water when skin diving. A diver should be alert to the possibility of dangerous marine life and growth. He should check with local skin diving groups for advice before diving in a new location.
- Avoid prolonged exposure to the water, particularly cold water. Fatigue and cold can cause cramps.
- Always stop, look up, reach up, and listen before surfacing after a dive.
- Do not allow small children to play with a mask while in the water. Lives have been lost because children, in placing the mask over their face, covered both the nose and mouth. With the mask in this position, the child's natural breathing creates a mask suction that cannot be released by the child, and he suffocates.
- Have a first aid kit available when skin diving. Gauze compresses, triangular bandages, adhesive compresses, scissors, and tweezers are a few of the items needed. All divers should complete a first aid course to learn how to care for injuries; local Red Cross chapters can provide this instruction.

RESCUE OF SCUBA DIVER

With the popularity of the sport of scuba diving, it is possible that a rescuer would be called upon to assist or rescue a scuba diver in trouble. Panic, exhaustion, cold exposure, serious injury, or unconsciousness may make such a rescue attempt necessary.

RESCUE TECHNIQUES

If the scuba diver is underwater, the rescuer should surface dive immediately and, upon reaching the diver, should first check the equipment that the victim is wearing. In cases when the victim is wearing a weight belt, the belt should be jettisoned by the rescuer's pulling on the quick-release buckle. If the victim is wearing an inflatable safety vest, the vest should be inflated as soon as possible. Inflation can be achieved by pulling on the lanyard that activates the self-contained capsule of compressed gas. Holding the victim's head back with one hand to insure an open airway, with the other hand the rescuer grasps the victim from behind at the armpit or by the first stage of the regulator or tank valve, and swims the diver to the surface. If the diver is wearing a vest that could not be inflated underwater, the rescuer can, when on the surface, inflate the vest by blowing into the inflation tube.

A victim who is already at the surface or one who has been brought up should be taken immediately to safety, using an appropriate tow. A tow, using the lifesaving stroke, can be carried out by grasping the regulator, by firmly grasping the collar of the vest, or by using the armpit tow.

IMMEDIATE FIRST AID

The immediate first aid step is to tow the scuba diving victim to a point where the victim can be removed from the water. The exception occurs when the shore or a boat is some distance away and the victim is not breathing or is bleeding severely. Severe bleeding can be stopped or controlled by applying direct pressure over the wound with the hand or, if bleeding is in an extremity, by applying pressure to the appropriate digital pressure point (see pages 199 through 202).

If the victim is not breathing, mouth-to-mouth respiration should be attempted, but only if either the rescuer or the victim has a buoyant aid to provide the necessary support (see page 194). As soon as possible, the rescuer should send for medical help. The victim should not be removed from the water without the use of a rigid support if an injury to the neck or back is suspected. After removal from the water, the victim should be treated for shock and exposure to cold water.

The U.S. Coast Guard maintains a Search and Rescue Service that can reach most locations quickly and can provide rapid transport of a victim to a hospital or to the nearest recompression facility when air embolism or decompression sickness is suspected.

7

THE JOB OF THE LIFEGUARD

The job of lifeguarding is not so glamorous or romantic as is often imagined. It is monotonous, exhausting work that is often misunderstood by lifeguards' employers and swimmers as well as the inexperienced lifeguard himself. Although a lifeguard's responsibilities and duties are many and varied and differ from facility to facility, the most important responsibility remains the same: to prevent accidents both in the water and on the immediate deck or beach area. The lifeguard's secondary responsibility is the rescue and emergency care of an accident victim. No other duty or responsibility can be allowed to interfere with these two functions.

QUALIFICATIONS

Each facility sets its own criteria for the qualifications of a lifeguard candidate, but every candidate should—
• Have obvious maturity of judgment
• Have a physical examination by a physician, attesting to good physical condition, good uncorrected vision, and normal hearing
• Hold current lifesaving and first aid certificates
• Pass a water test related to the facility to ensure the candidate's ability to perform

TRAINING

Initial Training

Before the candidate is assigned to lifeguard duty, the facility must train and orient the individual in the many aspects of his job and the characteristics of the facility. Such training and orientation should include information on the following subjects:
• The administrative structure of the facility
• Regulations for duty while assigned to the lifeguard stand, walking patrol, and water patrol

- The communication system
- The emergency plan
- Required uniforms
- The identification, location, and use of the facility's lifesaving and first aid equipment
- Swimmer rules and regulations
- Size, contour, depths, etc., of swimming areas
- Environmental conditions, danger areas, and hazards
- Facility schedule and operation

In-Service Training

Once a lifeguard is employed and initially trained, the person must maintain a constant high degree of mental alertness and physical condition. To attain and maintain this mental and physical "peak," the lifeguard must regularly swim, practice lifesaving and first aid skills, and review associated knowledge. Each facility should establish regularly scheduled in-service training sessions for all lifeguards. Examples of activities for increasing enthusiasm for these sessions are competition between lifeguards or with lifeguards of another facility, demonstrations for swimmers during break periods or as scheduled events, presentations of achievement awards, and participation in the Red Cross Swim and Stay Fit Program.

PREVENTIVE LIFEGUARDING

Carrying out the lifeguard's foremost responsibility, to prevent accidents, is called "preventive lifeguarding." Preventive lifeguarding takes many forms. Examples follow.

Enforcement of Rules

General rules for swimmer conduct should be simple, concise, and conspicuously posted. Proper and uniform enforcement of these rules will not only serve to protect the swimmers but also will enhance their enjoyment of the water and the facility. In addition to enforcing posted rules (Fig. 126), the lifeguard must use judgement in prohibiting any activity or practice that might endanger the participants or other swimmers. In making a decision, the lifeguard must recognize that while a particular practice may not endanger the participants, it may be unsafe for those who would try to emulate it or to other swimmers in the vicinity. A lifeguard's authority must not be questioned. The lifeguard must be the master

FIG. 126

of the situation at all times, sure of himself and steadfast in enforcing rules. The lifeguard must be tactful in handling disciplinary problems and must use self-restraint in language, temper, and manner. A system should be established by the facility for the removal of unruly swimmers from the swimming area.

Danger Areas and Hazards

There are danger areas and hazards common to all swimming facilities as well as those peculiar to each individual facility. Preventive lifeguarding requires identification of these areas and hazards, their elimination, swimmer avoidance, or constant surveillance of the known dangers.

Each facility should have a map or chart of the swimming area and immediate deck or beach area, on which the location of each accident that has occurred, either major or minor, is marked. The danger areas would soon be evident, and steps could be taken to protect the swimmers in those areas.

Common danger areas and related hazards are discussed below.

Entrance Areas

Swimmers rushing to the water may be in danger of slipping or being pushed. The result of enthusiasm and the desire to get into the water at the shallow depths may be that swimmers will dive or jump into water of insufficient depth; or weak swimmers or nonswimmers may jump into water over their heads.

Ladders

Ladders become a gathering place for swimmers. Weak swimmers or non-swimmers may be ducked at ladders or pushed to deep water. Depending upon the construction of the ladder, swimmers may become caught in a ladder or behind it, may slip and fall, or may use the upright as gymnastic equipment.

Blind Spots

The construction of the facility, location of the lifeguard stands, position of the sun, etc., can create spots in the swimming area that are difficult for the lifeguard to see. One frequently neglected area is directly under lifeguard stands that are close to the water's edge.

Overflows

There is a tendency for some weak swimmers or nonswimmers to "gutter around," or to work themselves into deep water by going hand over hand along the gutter or overflow system. This practice can also occur on open waterfronts where a pier or a lifeline enables swimmers to work themselves around into a dangerous area. In some pool overflow systems, young children may catch an elbow or a knee in the gutter and require assistance to be freed.

Diving Boards

Hazards can be minimized in diving areas by ruling that—
• Only one person is allowed on the board at a time (Fig. 127).
• One bounce is allowed per dive.

ONE DIVER
AT A TIME
ALLOWED ON
BOARD

FIG. 127

- All dives must be made from the front of the board, and water must have sufficient depth at entry point.
- No swimmers are allowed in the diving area.
- Divers must swim directly to an exit point before the next dive is allowed.

Slides

The hazards of slides are much like those of diving boards. Rules similar to those established for the diving area should be developed.

Marine Life

Marine life such as sharks, jellyfish, coral, and stingrays (see pages 23 through 26), present hazards that require special education and attention of the swimmers and lifeguards alike.

Rafts

Rafts can present several danger areas or hazards: one lifeguard cannot "guard" all four sides adequately; swimming to the raft is a challenge to the novice; rafts tip when overloaded; swimmers can become trapped while playing under the raft. Rafts should not have diving boards.

Step-offs

Areas of pools or waterfronts where the bottom dips sharply from shallow to deep water should have special attention from the lifeguard. Environmental conditions can change bottom contour of open waterfronts.

Observation of Water and Weather Conditions

Currents, wave action, clarity of water, storms, etc., create the need for special attention and procedures.

APPEARANCE

Uniform

All lifeguards should wear identifying apparel so that they can be easily located in case of an emergency. Studies have shown that while a swimmer merely in distress may call for help, an actively drowning person rarely does, and a passively drowning person cannot. The majority of drowning accidents are called to the attention of the lifeguard by another swimmer; therefore, the lifeguard must be readily identifiable. In addition, the lifeguard's uniform serves as protection from the elements. The lifeguard should wear a white sun helmet or hat to protect the head and face from the force of the sun. Polaroid-type sunglasses will protect the eyes from direct sunlight and glare. Jackets, T-shirts, warm-up suits, etc., are appropriate when the environment makes them necessary. All apparel should be readily identifiable.

Grooming

The lifeguard should be neatly groomed. Long hair must be affixed so as not to obscure vision or interfere with breathing while swimming. As much attention should be given to the appearance of the feet as to the appearance of the hands. Unnecessary jewelry, such as earrings, bracelets, and pins, should not be worn. The lifeguard should never listen to a radio, phonograph, or tape player, or read while on duty. The full attention of the lifeguard's eyes and ears must be directed toward protecting the swimmers. The lifeguard's appearance, dress, poise, and grooming have a direct bearing on the swimmers' confidence and on their respect for the lifeguard.

COMMUNICATIONS

Whistle

A loud, clear whistle is not only a part of the lifeguard's uniform but also is the means of immediate and emergency communication. It is used to fix the attention of the swimmers on the lifeguard for needed direction, to obtain the attention of another lifeguard, and to alert all personnel of danger or an emergency. The whistle should be used sparingly. Frequently, the attention of a swimmer may be caught merely through motions or voice. A whistle blown too often and for little purpose will soon be ignored. Each facility should establish necessary whistle signals, such as one short blast to gain the attention of a swimmer, two short blasts to gain the attention of another lifeguard, and one long blast to signal danger or emergency.

Hand Signals

In addition to the whistle, a set of standardized hand signals should be developed to further communicate with swimmers and with other lifeguards. Hand signals fall into three categories: giving direction to swimmers, transmitting information to other

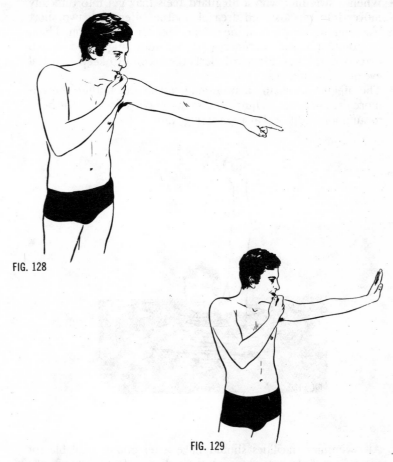

FIG. 128

FIG. 129

lifeguards, and requesting help or needed equipment. When the attention of the swimmers or of the other lifeguards is obtained by the whistle, the common practice of pointing directly at the individual concerned alerts the person to further signals or direction (Fig. 128).

The following three cases give examples of hand signal use:

• A person is preparing to dive from the 3-meter board when the lifeguard spots an underwater swimmer at the diver's entry point. The lifeguard quickly gives one short whistle blast to gain the attention of the diver and then, by pointing to the diver and extending the arm with the palm facing the diver, tells the diver to stop and stay where he is (Fig. 129).

- When a swimmer who a lifeguard feels may get into difficulty moves into the assigned area of another lifeguard, two short blasts on the whistle gain the second lifeguard's attention. Then, by pointing at the swimmer with the index finger and thumb extended, the first lifeguard alerts the second to keep a special eye on the swimmer.
- The lifeguard, making a swimming rescue and finding there is more than one victim, quickly raises a clenched fist over the head to summon additional assistance (Fig. 130).

FIG. 130

Telephone

All swimming facilities should have a telephone available for contacting ambulance personnel, the police, a doctor, etc., in the event of an emergency. A listing of emergency telephone numbers should be prominently displayed beside the telephone. If the facility is in a hard-to-find location, the facility should provide these emergency resource people with a map and directions prior to the opening and at least annually thereafter.

Additional Systems

Some facilities have additional communication systems such as two-way radios, public address systems, bullhorns, and flags. The lifeguard should fully understand the system used and should make use of it.

Equipment

Each facility must provide the lifeguard with needed lifesaving equipment related to the type of swimming area guarded. Examples of commonly used equipment are first aid kits, blankets, stretchers, backboards, reaching poles (shepherd's crooks), a rescue boat, a rescue paddleboard, ring buoys or heaving lines, rescue buoys (rescue tube, torpedo buoy), binoculars, masks, fins, and snorkles (see Chapter 2). Preventive lifeguarding requires that all equipment should be regularly checked and properly maintained in ready condition.

RELIEF BREAKS

It is not reasonable to assume that a lifeguard can maintain peak alertness hour after hour in the same position. Regularly scheduled breaks and rotation of assigned areas will relieve the lifeguard of monotony and boredom. One pattern of relief is a 10-minute break each hour and a rotation of assigned areas every 25 minutes. Whatever system is used, guards may never leave their assigned area until properly relieved.

NUMBER OF GUARDS

The number of lifeguards required will vary from facility to facility. Factors that help to determine the number of lifeguards needed are the experience and competence of the lifeguards; size, shape, and type of facility; and number of swimmers. There must be a sufficient number of lifeguards to adequately protect the swimmers, to allow for rest breaks, to provide coverage in case of emergency, and to substitute in case of absence or sudden illness.

CONDUCT

The importance of the lifeguard's conduct is apparent throughout this chapter. Whether on or off duty, the guard must set a good example and not indulge in any activity that is prohibited for swimmers or is in any way unsafe.

Important pointers for the lifeguard to observe are as follows:
- Report for duty on time, properly attired and groomed. Be in the assigned position when the shift starts.
- Maintain an erect posture and an alert attitude at all times.

- Refrain from unnecessary talk or visiting with swimmers or spectators. If talk is necessary, the lifeguard must continue to keep the assigned area under observation.
- Avoid engaging in any activity that will detract from constant surveillance of the swimmers.
- Avoid taking a "dip" unless specifically relieved for the purpose.
- Enforce all rules and prohibit unsafe activities.
- Be courteous, tactful, and poised.
- Discourage swimmers and other lifeguards from congregating around the lifeguard stand. The guard should remember that the lifeguard stand is an observation tower and is not to be used as a place where swimmers may leave their personal effects or children.
- While on walking patrol, move so as to be always facing the swimming area. The lifeguard could carry a light 10- or 12-foot pole or length of line, since these make excellent reaching assist devices.
- A group of swimmers must never be permitted to get between the lifeguard and the swimming area.
- While on water patrol in a boat or on a paddleboard, stay on the outer fringes of the bathing area and keep yourself (as much as possible) between the sun and the swimmers so that you may have a view without glare. Never allow swimmers to hang onto the boat or to swim around it.
- Be aware that you can be held liable for your actions or omissions of actions.

RESCUE AND EMERGENCY CARE

Despite the facility's precautions and the lifeguard's vigilance, swimmers do have accidents. The lifeguard must be thoroughly prepared and instantly ready to perform a rescue or render emergency care. In times of emergency, the poise and competent actions of the lifeguard can quell the fears and anxiety of the victim as well as those of other swimmers. The lifeguard should not dramatize any rescue or assist but quickly and in the most efficient manner perform the necessary actions.

Emergency Plan

No facility operation is complete without having a systematic procedure to follow in the event of a major accident. All personnel should be thoroughly trained in the prescribed emergency procedure and should have definite assigned duties. It is readily apparent, because of shift changes and rotating personnel, that all personnel must be familiar with all assignments and be capable of fitting into each assignment. The person in charge can then effectively issue directions with a minimum of confusion. Periodic practice sessions of the emergency plan should be conducted to assure the proper and efficient response of all personnel. The following points should be considered and included in an emergency plan:

- The emergency signal
- The actual rescue or emergency care of victims
- The obtaining of appropriate assistance such as additional lifeguards, rescue squad and ambulance personnel, the police, or a doctor
- The obtaining of needed equipment such as first aid supplies, a stretcher, backboards, blankets, or a resuscitator
- Search procedures for missing swimmers
- Supervision and control of other swimmers, either clearing the swimming area or restricting them to a "guarded" area of noninterference
- Accident reporting

First Aid

The majority of accidents at a swimming facility require first aid attention. Lifeguards will be confronted with swimmer conditions such as abrasions, lacerations, concussions, sunburn, and sudden illness. They should be prepared through training, equipment, and procedure to handle these and other emergencies, regardless of how minor they might be. In cases where the facility is some distance from the nearest medical aid, additional training in emergency care may be needed. In addition to having formal first aid training, the lifeguard should have a briefing by the facility's consulting physician on the handling of specific problems related to that facility.

Water Rescue

When a swimmer appears to be in trouble, the lifeguard must quickly analyze the situation to determine whether the swimmer is merely in distress or is actively drowning. The guard must then determine the most effective way to rescue or assist the swimmer. Whenever possible, the lifeguard should use a non-swimming rescue or assist from the shore, deck, or shallow water. If a swimming rescue is necessary, the guard immediately signals an emergency and makes the rescue with the use of an appropriate piece of equipment. The situation and the extent of injury will determine what steps of the emergency plan should be implemented.

8

SMALL CRAFT SAFETY

The term *small craft* is applied essentially to all categories of craft 25 feet and under in length. Most canoes, small sailing craft, outboard motorboats, inboard-outboard motorboats, small inboard motorboats, and craft propelled by oars are therefore in this category. Accidents, personal injuries, and fatalities in boating are more prevalent with these sizes and types of craft than with larger craft. The operators of small boats are usually found to be the principal cause of the majority of accidents with such craft. Collisions and capsizings account for over 70 percent of all accidents. The other leading types of accidents are fires and explosions, falls overboard, and groundings. Drownings continue to account for over 90 percent of fatalities sustained through boating.

Small craft are limited in their usage. Most are designed for a specific purpose and cannot safely perform a function they were not designed to perform. Wind and water conditions also limit the usage of small craft, as does the handling ability of the operator. A small boat must only be operated within safe limits to be safe.

PERSONAL SAFETY

Since drownings account for over 90 percent of the fatalities sustained in small craft accidents, it is necessary for anyone using a small boat to know how to swim in order to be reasonably safe while on the water. A good preliminary swimming test that an individual may apply to himself is — after pitching into the water, he should right himself and come to the surface and then stay afloat for 5 minutes by treading water, swimming with minimum progress, or resting in a floating position. This swim test should be accomplished while the individual is clothed, including shoes.

For those individuals who insist on going afloat even though they cannot swim, it is only prudent for them to *wear* a U.S. Coast Guard approved personal flotation device at all times while on the water.

It is recognized that any person, regardless of preventive measures, may, while afloat in a small craft, inadvertently find himself in the water. As an added measure of safety, all small craft users should practice putting on a personal flotation device while in the water and practice swimming with it. The yoke-type buoyancy vest is easily placed across the chest and under the arms, allowing a person to utilize a breast stroke for swimming to safety (Fig. 131). All such devices should be U.S. Coast Guard approved. However, small craft users should not overlook the use of improvised devices that may have to be used in an emergency.

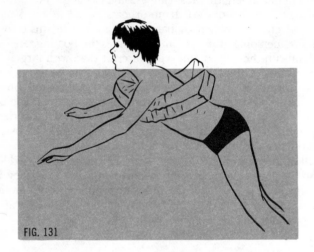

FIG. 131

CORRECT BOAT-HANDLING

To be reasonably safe in a small boat, a person must know how to properly operate the boat under a variety of conditions. This skill ability can only be developed through instruction and practical application of the necessary handling skills. There is no substitute for the knowledge, skill, and judgment developed through such an approach to learning safe boat operation. Where a boat will go and how it will behave are completely dependent on the correct use of its propulsion system, control system, and the existing conditions under which it is being operated. Presently there are several national organizations offering training in the safe operation of small craft:

American National Red Cross
U.S. Coast Guard Auxiliary
U.S. Power Squadrons
Boy Scouts of America
In addition, some states have small craft courses available to the public on request.

Due to the great growth in the field of boating and the problems related to this growth, there have been federal and state laws enacted to help safely regulate the activity. These laws attempt to assure boatmen safe enjoyment of the waterways. All persons venturing upon any waters today should well acquaint themselves with these regulations for the size and type of craft they are in and the waters they are on.

BOARDING AND DEBARKING

Procedures for correctly entering and leaving a small boat will differ somewhat, depending on the size and type of boat and how it is moored. There are, however, two fundamental principles of safety a person should apply: keep your center of gravity low and correctly distribute your weight (Fig. 132A).

When entering or leaving a craft alongside a pier, make sure the craft is secured at the bow and the stern. The bow and stern lines should be snug but not so tight that they will hinder the boat from settling when weight is added or when the tide goes out. Wear nonskid deck shoes and appropriate clothing. Enter the boat at or near amidships and take care not to pinch your fingers between the boat's gunwale (side) and the pier as you grasp the gunwale with the hand nearest the boat. Step aboard as near as possible to the centerline of the boat. Shift your hands and grasp both gunwales as your weight is transferred to the foot in the boat (Fig. 132B). Then

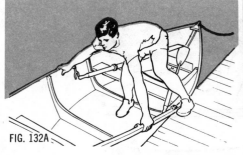

FIG. 132A

FIG. 132B

bring the other foot aboard. When leaving the craft, simply reverse the entire procedure. Leaving the craft poses no problems as long as the mooring lines are secured.

Prior to entering the boat, check for waves or for wakes of passing boats. An unexpected movement of the boat due to wave action, at the moment you step aboard, may prove quite hazardous. Always make sure you do not step on any equipment within the boat. It may not be secured and could cause you to lose your footing.

When boarding or debarking from a beach or shoreline, first make sure the craft is completely waterborne, but barely so. To enter, step over the bow (or stern), placing one foot along the centerline as both hands grasp the gunwales (Fig. 133A). The boat will be held to the beach when the body weight is shifted to the foot in the boat. Keep the weight low as the other foot is brought aboard.

FIG. 133A

FIG. 133B

As the weight is shifted toward the other end of the craft, the
beached end will lift free (Fig. 133B). This procedure is reversed
when you debark at a beach or shoreline. Always wear protective
footgear when boarding or debarking at a beach or shoreline.

LOADING AND TRIMMING

Small boats are somewhat limited in their safe load carrying
abilities. If the craft does not have a capacity rating plate, it may be
operated on the principle of one person per seat (or thwart). Or it
should have a minimum of 6 inches of freeboard in calm water.

In other words, the gunwales at their lowest point should be 6
inches above the water when the boat is fully loaded. Under adverse
conditions, of weather and water, more freeboard is required for
safe operation.

Any small boat or canoe that is handled with more difficulty than
usual and responds sluggishly and is difficult to trim is overloaded.

A small craft operator should never assume that passengers know
how to properly enter, leave, or handle themselves in a small boat.
The craft must be steadied and the passengers must be assisted by
being told where to step, sit, etc. All gear should be handed into the
craft and stowed so as not to interfere with the operation of the
craft until time for usage of the equipment is at hand.

Trimming a craft is simply a matter of placing the weight of all
gear and passengers so that the craft is balanced from side to side
and fore and aft. All weight should center amidships. Once the craft
is underway, slight adjustments in fore-and-aft and side-to-side
trim may be made to determine the best trim for safe, smooth,
efficient operation. Any tendency for the bow to ride lower than the
stern or vice versa indicates a hazardous condition that must
promptly be corrected. If the bow is lower than the stern, some
weight should be moved aft; if the stern is low, some weight should
be moved forward. (Only enough weight should be moved to obtain
a balance.) If the craft is not trimmed properly from side to side it
will lean to the heavy side. Improper load distribution (trim), unless
corrected, can cause loss of control.

CHANGING POSITIONS

There is rarely a need to change positions in a small boat. If such
a need arises, there are several basic principles that should be
observed:

- Only one person should move at a time.
- The weight should be kept low and as near the center of the craft as possible.
- The boat should be kept trimmed by the occupants' balancing the weight of one occupant with the weight of another.
- In undesirable conditions such as heavy wave action, it is not advisable to attempt the changing of positions. If such changing is necessary, the principles shown above should be followed.

SELF-RESCUE IN A CAPSIZE OR SWAMPING SITUATION

Most all modern small craft, regardless of the type of materials used for construction, are designed to float when filled with water. Floating positions of swamped or capsized craft will vary, depending on (1) where the flotation material is located, (2) how much flotation material is used, and (3) how much weight is on the transom (after part of the hull) in the form of a motor. If the craft floats either in an upright position or inverted position, the built-in flotation allows the craft to be used as means of saving the lives of its occupants.

An overturned or a swamped craft offers two means of self-rescue:

(1) If the craft is in the overturned position, the victims may hold onto the hull and swim it ashore or hold onto the hull and wait until assistance arrives (Fig. 134). If the victim is alone, he may place a portion of his weight on the hull and slowly kick his way to safety if the craft is small in size. In a larger craft, the victim should conserve his energy and wait for assistance. When there is more than one victim, it is advisable for victims to arrange themselves along each side of the hull and hold onto it. This method allows swimming the craft, in the overturned position, to safety. If one victim becomes fatigued, the victims may grasp each other's wrists across the keel and rest.

(2) If the craft is in a righted swamped position, the victims may enter the craft from opposite sides by placing their hands in the bottom of the craft, kicking their feet to the surface, and swimming into the craft (Fig. 135). When the hips clear the gunwale, the person entering should roll into a sitting position and balance the craft from side to side as well as from bow to stern. When this position is gained, the victims may hand paddle the craft to safety (Fig. 136). This method is preferable to clinging to an upright hull; however, some craft will not float in an upright swamped position.

G. 134

135

G. 136

Victims should always stay with the boat unless it is being carried toward potentially dangerous areas such as waterfalls, dams, or water intakes for hydroelectric power plants. It is much easier for rescuers to locate a boat in distress than to spot an individual. However, if water temperatures are extremely cold, if the victims are able to swim, and if safety is relatively close, it may be advisable to attempt swimming to safety. Otherwise, the victim should try to right the boat and get aboard. Aboard the boat, with a U.S. Coast Guard personal flotation device (PFD) being worn, a victim has his best opportunity for survival.

RULES OF THE ROAD

The purpose of the "Rules of the Road" is to prevent accidents by establishing certain procedures that boats must follow when danger of collision exists. These rules require motorized craft to give the right of way to manually propelled craft and sailboats (the one exception to this rule is that of a sailboat overtaking a motorboat). These "Rules of the Road" may be found in U.S. Coast Guard publications CG 169, CG 172, and CG 184. Operating rules for the Great Lakes, western rivers, and inland and international waters are similar to each other in most respects, but the boatmen should always follow the specific rules for the area they are in.

Manually propelled craft, although having the right of way over power craft, should exercise caution and avoid practices that may confuse other boat operators or cause a dangerous situation to develop. Regardless of who has the right of way, operators of all craft are responsible for taking *all necessary action* to avoid collision.

The situations on the following page (meeting, crossing, and passing) and the actions to be taken are based upon the Inland Rules.

EQUIPMENT

Boat owners and operators should determine whether their state regulations differ from those of the federal government, but in all instances in the chart on page 148, only the *minimum* equipment required by law is listed. Additional gear is needed for safety and convenience.

Additional equipment that may be needed for safety is usually based on what the craft will be used for and on special needs of the operator. A minimum amount of such equipment would include bow and stern lines, a bailer, a light anchor, extra oars or paddles, and a first aid kit. Boat operators should remember that a Coast Guard approved personal flotation device (PFD) is required to be aboard for each occupant.

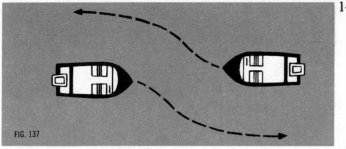

FIG. 137

Meeting When meeting each other head on or nearly so, boats should keep to their right. The rule is the same as the corresponding traffic rule for automobiles.

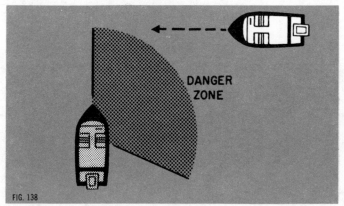

DANGER ZONE

FIG. 138

Crossing In a crossing situation, the boat on the right is the privileged vessel. The boat on the left is the burdened vessel and must slow down, change course, and pass astern of the other boat. It may be necessary at times for the burdened boat to stop or reverse to avoid collision.

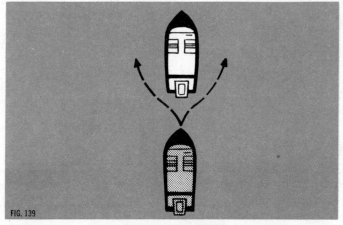

FIG. 139

Passing In a passing situation, the boat being overtaken is the privileged vessel. The passing (burdened) boat may pass on either side after proper signals have been exchanged and must keep clear.

FEDERALLY REQUIRED EQUIPMENT

(Listed below is the minimum federally required equipment for small boats in use in the United States)

Equipment	Class A (Less than 16 feet)	Class 1 (16 feet to less than 26 feet)	Class 2 (26 feet to less than 40 feet)	Class 3 (40 feet to not more than 65 feet)
Back-Fire Flame Arrester	One approved device on each carburetor of all gasoline engines installed after April 25, 1940, except outboard motors.			
Ventilation	At least two ventilator ducts (at least one exhaust duct installed so as to extend from the open atmosphere to the lower portion of the bilge and at least one intake duct installed so as to extend to a point at least midway to the bilge or at least below the level of the carburetor air intake). These ducts must be fitted with cowls or their equivalent for the purpose of properly and efficiently ventilating the bilges of every engine and fuel tank compartment of boats constructed or decked over after April 25, 1940, using gasoline or other fuel of a flashpoint less than 110°F. The cowls shall be located and trimmed for maximum effectiveness and in such a manner so as to prevent displaced fumes from being recirculated.			
Bell	None*	None*	One, which when struck produces a clear, bell-like tone of full, round characteristics.	
Personal Flotation Devices (PFD's) (Wearable devices must be of suitable size.)	All recreational boats less than 16 feet in length, all canoes and kayaks must have one Type I, II, III, or IV PFD for each person on board.	All recreational boats 16 feet or over in length must have one Type I, II, or III (wearable) for each person on board plus one Type IV (throwable) in each boat. The Type I, II, or III devices shall be immediately available for use.		
Whistle	None*	One, hand-, mouth- or power-operated audible at least ½ mile and capable of producing a blast of 2 seconds or more duration.	One, hand- or power-operated, audible at least 1 mile, capable of producing a blast of 2 seconds or more duration.	One, power-operated audible at least 1 mile, capable of producing a blast of 2 seconds or more duration.
Fire Extinguisher, Portable (When NO fixed fire extinguishing system is installed in machinery spaces.)	None*	At least one B-I Type approved hand-portable fire extinguisher (not required on outboard motorboats less than 26 feet in length and not carrying passengers for hire if the construction of such motorboats will not permit the entrapment of explosive or flammable gases or vapors.)	At least two B-I Type approved hand-portable fire extinguishers, OR at least one B-II Type approved hand-portable fire extinguisher.	At least three B-I Type approved hand-portable fire extinguishers; or at least one B-I Type plus one B-II Type approved hand-portable fire extinguisher.
(When fixed fire extinguishing system is installed in machinery spaces.)	None*		At least one B-I Type approved hand-portable fire extinguisher.	At least two B-I Type approved hand-portable fire extinguishers; or at least one B-II Type approved hand-portable fire extinguisher.
	B-I Type approved hand-portable fire extinguishers contain: foam, 1¼ up to 2½ gallons; or carbon dioxide, 4 up to 15 pounds; or dry chemical, 2 up to 10 pounds; or Freon, 2½ to 4 pounds. B-II Type approved hand-portable fire extinguishers contain: foam 2½ up to 12 gallons; or carbon dioxide, 15 to 35 pounds; or dry chemical, 10 up to 20 pounds.			
Pollution Control	(1) All vessels under 100-ton gross must have a fixed or portable means to discharge oily bilge slops to a reception facility. A bucket or bailer is considered a portable means. (2) No person may drain the sumps of oil-lubricated machinery or the contents of oil filters, strainers, or purifiers into the bilge of any U.S. vessel.		(1) Same as Class A and Class I (2) Same as Class A and Class I (3) Vessels 26 feet in length or over must have posted a placard at least 5 x 8 inches—made of durable material, fixed in a conspicuous place in the machinery spaces, or at the bilge and ballast pump control station giving the statement below.	
	Discharge of oil prohibited—The Federal Water Pollution Control Act prohibits the discharge of oil or oily waste into or upon the navigable waters and contiguous zone of the United States if such discharge causes a film or sheen upon, or discoloration of, the surface of the water, or causes a sludge or emulsion beneath the surface of the water. Violators are subject to a penalty of $5,000.			

*Not required by Motorboat Act of 1940. However, the "Rules of the Road" require these vessels to sound proper signals.

At no time should an individual attempt to use a craft whose hull or equipment is in a poor state of repair. It is also imperative for the operator of any craft to have a complete working knowledge of that craft and all of its equipment.

SMALL CRAFT USE IN RESCUE

In planning and carrying out a rescue, operators of small craft must take into account the circumstances and conditions that exist at the time the rescue is attempted. Trained operators of rescue craft are always able to initiate a course of action that minimizes the risks involved in the rescue operation. All equipment must be in top condition and ready for instant use. Essentially, either of two basic rescue procedures should be employed.

(1) A flotation device is tossed or extended to the victim while the craft is made dead in the water. The victim swims with the flotation device, or is pulled, to the safety of the rescue craft.

(2) A flotation device is tossed to the victim and the craft is maneuvered to enable the rescuer to make contact with the victim.

Although these procedures are sound, they must be considered in relation to the type of craft used. With a manually propelled craft, the approach to the victim is made against the wind or the current (whichever is stronger). When the craft is in close proximity to the victim, the operator holds the craft in position while the victim is assisted or rescues himself. If the freeboard is too high or the victim is too heavy, the victim may need assistance from a physically able person. By going overboard and suspending himself full length from the transom or gunwale, the rescuer can have his shoulders used as a step by the victim to enter the boat (Fig. 141). If the victim is unconscious or unable to assist himself, the rescue craft must approach the victim as approaching a mooring and make contact with him on the downwind, downstream, or downcurrent side forward of amidships. The rescuer can then bring the victim aboard by lifting him and jackknifing him at his hips over the transom or gunwale (Figs. 142A through C). The victim's legs can then be swung aboard.

Motorized rescue craft use the same rescue techniques as manually operated craft, with little adaptation. Two conditions, however, create an element of danger in effecting rescues with motorized craft: the speeds at which such craft operate and the unguarded propeller.

Motorized rescue craft should approach the victim at greatly

FIG. 141

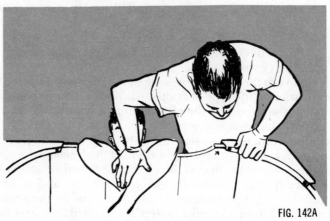

FIG. 142A

reduced speed, and the rescuer should make contact with the victim from the downwind or downcurrent side and forward of amidships. Prior to contact, the motor should be stopped. In many small, motorized craft, placing the motor in neutral does not assure stopping the spinning action of the propeller. It is therefore best to stop the motor and allow the craft to coast or drift the last few feet to the victim.

FIG. 142B

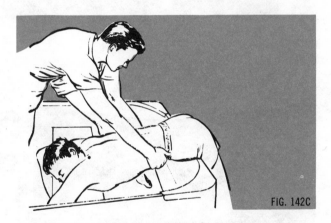

FIG. 142C

LOCATIONS OF LIFEBOATS AT A WATERFRONT

The proper placement of lifeboats at a swimming water-front depends on the swimming load, how the area is physically arranged, what the water conditions are, and the type of craft to be used in the rescue operation.

Following are diagrams of several fresh-water waterfronts with proper positioning of lifeboats when the waterfront is in use and when not in use. These diagrams are based on maximum utilization of the waterfront.

Fresh-Water Camps

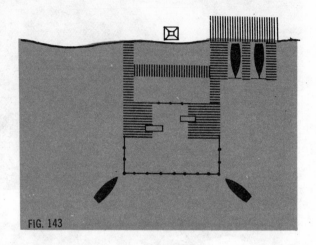

"LL" Dock

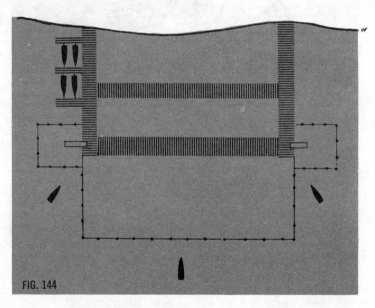

"A" Dock

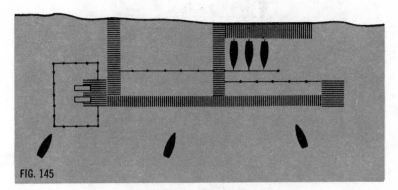

"Double T" Dock

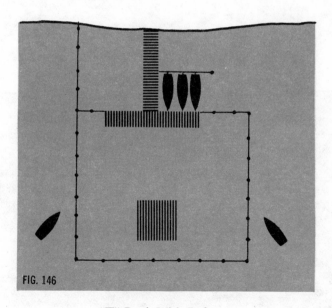

"T" Dock With Raft

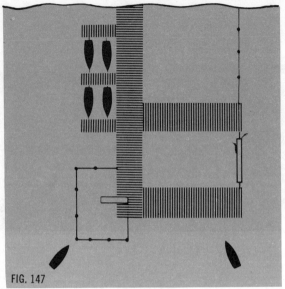

FIG. 147

"F" Dock

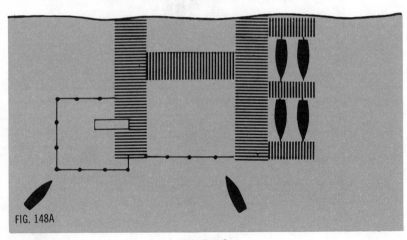

FIG. 148A

"H" Dock

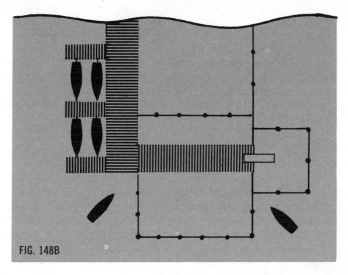

FIG. 148B

"L" Dock

Salt-Water Camps With Enclosed Beachfront

At surf beaches, proper placement of lifeboats and their utilization are affected by the same factors as for fresh- and salt-water waterfronts. However, due to somewhat simplified physical arrangements, lifeboats at surf beaches are either located strategically along the beach, ready for instant use, or are on patrol parallel to the beach beyond the surf line. The number and type of boats utilized will depend on local conditions and preferences of beach management.

9

ICE SAFETY AND RESCUE

The winter season provides opportunities for engaging in a variety of sports activities, and, unfortunately, increases the likelihood of a variety of sports-related accidents also. Even in the extreme northern United States, where the coming of ice is a normal annual event and ice skating and hockey are daily winter sports, hazardous conditions are not always recognized, and accidents do happen. Through recklessness, carelessness, or lack of knowledge, hundreds of people accidentally break through ice each year, and some are drowned.

Safety in ice skating depends largely on two kinds of knowledge: where a person may skate safely and under what conditions.

WHERE TO SKATE

Small bodies of water such as ponds, slowly flowing streams, and small lakes generally offer the safest conditions for out-of-doors skating. These freeze more quickly than larger bodies of water, and the ice formed is generally smoother and remains longer.

Ice formed over swiftly moving water, or where water level is apt to change, is likely to be unsafe no matter how thick.

SAFE CONDITIONS FOR SKATING

Unfortunately, there is no one rule that can be applied to ensure skating safety under all conditions. In general, ice may be considered on the basis of age. Newly formed ice is often referred to as young ice. Ice that is firm and solid, as it is during a prolonged freeze, is known simply as good or firm ice. Thawing ice is usually called old or rotten ice.

Young ice formed during the first freeze is tough and elastic and may crack in all directions yet still support a small person. However, young ice is unsafe until it has frozen to a thickness of at least 2 inches, and even then it may not support a group. Ice must freeze to a uniform depth of 4 inches before it is the firm ice that is safe for group skating. The old ice of spring that has been subjected to thaws is never safe for ice sports.

ICE ACCIDENTS AND SELF-RESCUE

There are at least two general rules that apply in all cases in which a person breaks through ice: (1) the person should not attempt to climb out immediately and (2) the victim should kick his feet to the surface to the rear to avoid jackknifing the body beneath the ice rim. Rather than follow the first impulse to climb out after breaking through the ice, the person should extend the hands and arms forward on the unbroken surface, kick to nearly level position, and attempt to work forward onto the ice (Fig. 149). If the ice breaks

FIG. 149

again, the victim should maintain this position and slide forward again. The victim, upon reaching firm ice, should not immediately stand but should roll away from the break area, thus distributing the weight over as broad an area as possible on the weak ice.

RESCUE WITH EQUIPMENT

Too often, when someone falls through ice, a would-be rescuer also breaks the ice in attempting to assist. Any equipment that helps distribute the weight of rescuers across a broader area of ice will alleviate this problem. One of the most useful devices for ice rescue is a light ladder, from 14 to 18 feet long, with a light, strong line attached to the lowest rung. The ladder should be shoved out on the ice to the limit of its length, with the line serving as an extension. If able to do so, the victim can climb onto the ladder and move along its length in a prone position.

FIG. 150

If the victim is unable to climb onto the ladder, the rescuer may crawl out on the ladder to assist (Fig. 150). If the ice breaks under the ladder, the ladder will angle upward from the broken ice area and can be drawn to safety by other persons.

For rescues in which the rescuer must remain at a distance from the victim because of ice conditions, a ring buoy with line attached or a coiled line with a weighted end may be thrown to the victim. A ring buoy can be scaled along the ice for a considerable distance.

A hockey stick with line attached can also be scaled along the ice. Sometimes a tree branch or board may be the only available device (Figs. 151 and 152). A spare tire, preferably with line attached, may be used for an extension rescue and will support several people.

FIG. 151

FIG. 152

FIG. 153

An "ice cross" (Fig. 153), constructed of 8-foot 2 by 4's with line attached, will distribute weight over a wide area and prevent the ice from giving way as the victim is pulled to safety.

In addition, a victim of ice accident may be rescued by use of a small flat-bottom boat shoved along the ice (Fig. 154). The victim is pulled aboard over the stern.

FIG. 154

FIG. 155

OTHER MEANS OF RESCUE

Where no regular or improvised rescue devices are available, it may be necessary to form a human chain to effect a rescue. To form this chain, several rescuers approach as closely as they can with safety and then lie prone upon the ice, forming a "chain" (Fig. 155). Each person holds tightly to the skates or ankles of the person ahead of him. If possible, the lightest person should be closest to the victim. When the lead person grasps the victim, the person nearest shore pulls the others back. If the ice breaks under the weight of the leading person in the chain, the individual can be held and drawn to safety by the others.

CARE OF ICE-ACCIDENT VICTIMS

Victims of skating and ice accidents may require artificial respiration, which should be administered on the way to shelter, as well as warming and treatment for shock. If the victim is not breathing, mouth-to-mouth respiration should be started immediately and should be given during transport.

When the victim is brought to shore breathing, first aid treatment for cold exposure is needed.

The rescuers should—

1. Bring the victim indoors as soon as possible
2. Warm the victim as rapidly as possible
3. Remove the wet clothing and wrap the victim in blankets until it is possible to immerse the person in warm water (102° to 105° F)

Victims of lengthy immersions in cold water should always be seen by a physician.

10

SURVIVAL SWIMMING IN CIVILIAN EMERGENCIES

Drownings can occur anyplace where there is water. In fact, National Safety Council statistics on drownings around the home show that individuals have drowned in bathtubs, wells, cisterns, and even accumulated rainwater and other casual water as well as in swimming pools. Only about 40 percent of the yearly drownings occur to people who are swimming or playing in the water. The remaining 60 percent are nonswimming fatalities due to accidentally falling into the water from piers, decks of pools, bridges, shores, and recreational boats, and while fishing or hunting.

It can readily be understood, then, that a great number of drownings occur among campers, fishermen, hunters, and boaters, who have no intention of entering the water. When they unexpectedly find themselves in the water fully clothed, they tend to panic and drown unless assistance is near at hand. Some experience in swimming and floating fully clothed, removing clothing in water when necessary, and inflating clothing may prevent panic and save a life in an aquatic emergency.

BASIC SKILLS

Current information and basic skills taught in survival swimming are the result of extensive inquiry and experimental work. Starting in World War II, thousands of members of the armed forces were taught the basic elements of how to survive in the water. As a result, it has been possible to determine and refine the skills most essential for survival under military conditions. There is a need, however, for the millions of civilians who participate in any activity on, near, or about the water to also learn basic aquatic skills for survival.

All of the skills included in this chapter are described in detail in Red Cross water safety textbooks and instructor manuals. Emphasis in survival swimming, therefore, will be placed on necessary adaptations involved to survive when fully clothed.

Breath Control

Breath control is a key to survival. The swimmer must first learn to be able to take a deep breath, submerge, and hold the breath below the surface (Fig. 156). Repeated practice will enable the individual to lengthen the time during which he or she can comfortably stay underwater.

Rhythmic breathing consists of inhaling through the mouth while just above the surface and exhaling through both mouth and nose below the surface. Practice can originate in shoulder-depth water and be repeated until the swimmer can repeat the procedure with ease for at least 50 times.

FIG. 156

Bobbing

Bobbing consists of a rhythmic breathing exercise in water over one's own depth. Constant practice can make this skill a valuable breath control and survival skill. Forward progress can be made by inhaling at the surface, submerging to the bottom, and pushing off at a forward angle, all the while exhaling through mouth and nose.

Floating for Survival

The ability to remain afloat with little or no effort for an extended period of time will enable the victim of a water accident to increase survival time.

Back Floating

Most swimmers will float on the back position with little effort (Fig. 157). Assuming a comfortable position, the swimmer should experiment to determine minimum effort required to stay in this resting position. Gentle sculling or finning action of the arms, with slight kicking, may be helpful in maintaining a back floating position. Breath control is important, since many swimmers will float more easily when their lungs are full; therefore, maximum lung volume can be maintained by periods of normal breath-holding followed by rapid exhalation and inhalation.

FIG. 157

Survival Floating, Face Down

The face-down floating technique combines a series of basic skills and can keep a person afloat for a long period with a minimum of effort and energy expended. It is adapted from the technique called "drownproofing," which was originated by the late Fred R. Lanoue, former professor of physical education and head swimming coach at the Georgia Institute of Technology. This technique takes advantage of the fact that with the face-down position in the water, the body will usually swing into a semivertical position, but the face and head will remain just below the surface, thus requiring little movement or energy to raise the face high enough to breathe. The skill of survival floating can be performed as described below.

Resting Position

The swimmer starts with air in the lungs and holds the breath, letting the arms and legs dangle (Fig. 158 A). The face is kept down so that the back of the head is at the surface. The swimmer rests and floats in this vertical position for a few seconds.

Preparing To Exhale

While maintaining this body and head position, the swimmer slowly and leisurely recovers, or lifts the arms to about shoulder height (Fig. 158 B). If leg action is also to be used, the swimmer slowly separates the legs into a modified scissors kick.

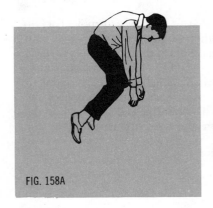

FIG. 158A

FIG. 158B

FIG. 158C

Exhalation

Making sure that the back of the head is still at the surface, the swimmer raises the head no higher than necessary for the mouth to clear the surface (Fig. 158 C). At the same time the individual exhales through the mouth and nose (some may exhale through mouth only or nose only). The eyes should be opened to help gauge and judge the head and body levels.

Inhalation

As soon as the head is vertical, the swimmer presses the arms downward and brings the legs together (Fig. 158 D). This easy downward pressure should allow time for air to be breathed in through the mouth. The action of the arms and legs should not be vigorous enough to lift the chin out of the water.

Return to the Resting Position

The swimmer slowly allows the arms and legs to move back to their free-dangling position, with face down in the water, and relaxes (Fig. 158 E). The individual rests in this position until ready to exhale and then repeats the cycle. NOTE. If the individual tends to sink too far below the surface when going back to the dangling or resting position, a downward press or easy finning action of the arms will stop the sinking of the body and help float it back to the surface. A slight scissors kick can also be combined to arrest the sinking action.

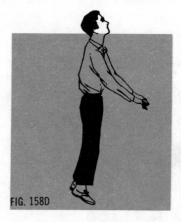

FIG. 158D

FIG. 158E

SWIMMING FULLY CLOTHED

When it is necessary to make progress through the water while fully clothed, the only practical strokes are those that employ an underwater recovery of the arms. The weight of the water-soaked clothing makes it impractical to use any stroke that demands an out-of-water recovery. To survive and, when necessary, to swim to safety, the swimmer should use one or a combination of the following underwater arm recovery strokes.

Breaststroke

This stroke utilizes a body position in which the head can be kept slightly up for continuous breathing or the face may be lowered for exhalation. The arms stay under the surface and the press back is somewhat down and back to a point just in front of the shoulders, and then the arms are recovered forward. For survival purposes, the kick could be a modified scissors kick with the length of glide minimized. The breaststroke is a good stroke and skill to have if it is necessary to help someone in distress.

Sidestroke

This stroke uses the effective scissors kick and underwater action of the arms. The side position enables the swimmer to carry the face clear of the water for ease of continuous breathing. The glide would be minimized, and this stroke is the basic one for towing a victim in distress.

Elementary Backstroke

This is a good changeover stroke from either the breaststroke or sidestroke when necessary to make progress and conserve energy. All movements occur underwater, and with the face up, continued free breathing is another advantage. For survival, the important element is ease of performance rather than technique; therefore, depending on the swimmer's skill, the glide can be shortened or lengthened and the kick can be a scissors or inverted scissors kick if the swimmer is not adept at doing a breaststroke kick.

Treading Water

In this skill, the swimmer is in a vertical position and is submerged to the chin. The arm action is a sculling motion, pressing downward against the water. The legs should be doing the most effective and strongest kick for the particular individual: a breaststroke, scissors, or rotary. The skill of treading is essential in making flotation gear out of shirt, slacks, seabags, etc. It keeps the swimmer in an effective upright position when the swimmer is signaling for help, awaiting rescue, or maintaining visual contact with a victim.

SUBMERGING AND SWIMMING UNDERWATER

These skills may be necessary when a swimmer must go to the assistance of a submerged victim or must quickly submerge in order to avoid being run down by an oncoming craft.

Submerging

To submerge quickly from the vertical, or treading water, position, the feetfirst surface dive is most effective. From this position, a vigorous scissors or breaststroke kick is given, and at the same time, the arms are pressed downward against the water. These actions will raise the swimmer as far out of the water as possible. As the weight of the unsupported body drives the swimmer below the surface, the hands, with palms up, are swept up in a wide arc to an overhead position, thus adding to the downward momentum. At the required depth, the swimmer levels off and swims forward.

Swimming Underwater

For swimming underwater, an adaptation of the breaststroke is generally the easiest and most efficient method. It is recommended that swimmers use full arm action, pulling right through to the thighs, followed by the kick and a glide with arms by the sides, to obtain maximum glide from each movement.

Original practice in underwater swimming should be limited to about 20 or 25 feet and extended only after several practice sessions. Practice in underwater swimming must be done only under the surveillance of a qualified instructor or guard.

Hyperventilation

Swimmers with average skill rarely swim at depths greater than from 10 to 15 feet and should not go deeper except to perform an emergency rescue or, after long practice, to engage in skin diving or other underwater activities. Distance underwater swimming should be discouraged, and the dangers of hyperventilating the lungs before swimming underwater should be thoroughly understood. Hyperventilation, or deep breathing, increases breath-holding time by blowing off carbon dioxide and thus lowering the amount of carbon dioxide in the blood. If, following hyperventilation, the swimmer attempts to swim underwater for a distance, a considerable length of time may elapse before the carbon dioxide level, reduced by overbreathing, will provide a strong stimulus to breathe. The danger is that the oxygen level may drop to a point where the swimmer "blacks out" before the carbon dioxide level increases to the point where the individual feels the urge to take a breath. Unless help is at hand to get the swimmer to the surface, drowning will result. Every person engaged in underwater swimming should be paired with a buddy and should be closely supervised.

ENTRY FROM A HEIGHT

Since it may be necessary to enter the water from any reasonable height with a maximum of safety, the swimmer must use judgment to determine the best method of entry. Headfirst entry should be attempted only by those experienced in diving, and then only when depth of water is known to be adequate, and water is clear of obstructions. If any doubt exists, the feetfirst entry should be made, and if obstacles are encountered, chances of survival are much greater.

Jumping

When a person jumps from a height, the simplest technique is to look straight ahead, step forward with one foot, and quickly bring the other one up to it. The body is held straight, and entry is made with feet together and hands on thighs.

Leaning forward or backward on takeoff can be dangerous, since once a person is in the air, the momentum is difficult to stop, and serious injury can result if the person lands at an angle. To lessen the depth of penetration and to soften possible hitting of the bottom, the jumper can, immediately after contact, let the legs bend at the knees. If not a practiced jumper from a height, the person may grasp the nose with one hand and hold the opposite shoulder with the free hand over the hand holding the nose to prevent injury to the face upon impact with the water.

Jumping From a Height Wearing a PFD

Wearing a personal flotation device (PFD), an individual should cross the arms against the device, holding it tightly to the chest and down from the shoulders. This action will prevent water from gushing up between the body and the device, causing the straps to be torn off and the device to be lost as the body hits the water.

DISROBING IN THE WATER

A majority of drownings occur to people who find themselves accidentally in the water and fully clothed. In such cases the knowledge of how to disrobe in the water can be vitally important. The weight of water-soaked clothing impairs swimming efficiency, but in some instances it might be best not to disrobe. When safety is only a short distance away or there is the problem of cold water or when it is possible to safely hang onto a buoyant object, it might not be advisable to disrobe.

If the swimmer realizes that shirts and slacks can be easily inflated and can act as flotation supports, it is readily seen that there is no need for panic. First of all, however, the shoes should be removed (Fig. 159). To accomplish this, the swimmer takes a good breath and assumes a jellyfish float position. Then, using both hands, the person removes one shoe at a time. When necessary, the head should be lifted long enough to take additional breaths as needed during this procedure.

FIG. 159

USE OF CLOTHING FOR FLOTATION

Close-woven materials that most shirts and slacks are made from hold trapped air when wet.

Shirts

The shirt can be inflated to give initial support. First, the shirt is buttoned at the collar and made tight at the neck (Fig. 160A). Then the swimmer takes a deep breath, bends the head forward, pulls the shirt up to the face, and exhales between the second and third buttons (Fig. 160B). The air will rise and form a bubble at the back of the shirt and give the needed support. The shirttail ends should be tied together at the waist, and, in addition, it may be necessary to grasp the shirt collar tightly to prevent the escape of the trapped air.

FIG. 160A

FIG. 160B

Another method of inflating a shirt is by splashing air into it with the palm of the hand. To accomplish this skill, the swimmer floats on the back and holds the front of the shirttail with one hand, keeping it just under the surface. The free hand strikes downward from above the surface with the palm and continues the motion to a point below the shirttail. The air, carried downward from the surface, will bubble into the shirt, causing the inflation.

Slacks

To use slacks for flotation, the swimmer takes a good breath, assumes a jellyfish float position, loosens the waistband or belt, and carefully and easily removes one leg of the clothing at a time (Fig. 161A). The head should be lifted high enough to take a breath as often as may be necessary. It is important not to hurry.

After the slacks are removed, the swimmer treads water and either ties both legs of the slacks together at the cuff or ties a knot in each leg as close to the bottom of the leg as possible. Then, with the zipper pulled up, the swimmer grasps the back of the waistband with one hand and, with the slacks on the surface, splashes air into the open waist with the free hand (Fig. 161B). This action is easily accomplished by striking down with the palm and following through to a point just below the open waist, which is kept below the surface.

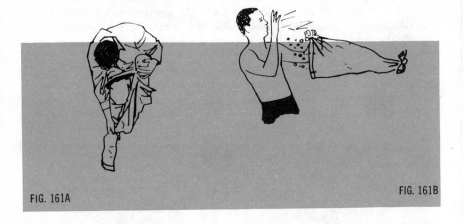

FIG. 161A   FIG. 161B

Another simple method of inflating slacks is to submerge and blow air into them through the waistband, which should be kept underwater. After the slacks have been inflated, the waistband can be gathered together by the hands or by tightening the belt if there is one.

The swimmer can then slip the head between the legs of the slacks near where they have been tied together, thus forming a Mae West type of flotation (Fig. 162). If the legs are tied separately, the swimmer uses the inflated slacks as water wings, which would be an equally serviceable improvised flotation support.

Skirts

A skirt, or the lower part of a dress, can best be used if it is kept on. The swimmer lies in a back horizontal floating position and then

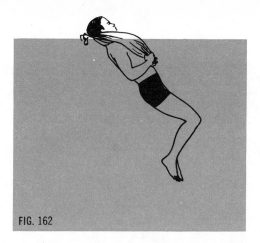

FIG. 162

uses the hem to scoop, in a semicircular fashion, away from the body to trap air. The hem is curled in underneath and held down to retain the resulting bubble of air.

FLOTATION WITH WADERS OR
RUBBER FOOTWEAR

Hunting and fishing enthusiasts wearing full outdoor gear that includes hip boots, waders, or rubber boots usually panic when they fall into the water, since the common impression is that they will be pulled to the bottom. This is a fallacy.

When a person so clad falls into the water headfirst, air is usually trapped in the boots. By relaxing, the person will be pulled to the surface in a moment, with the feet coming up first. By slowly raising the head, keeping the body in a horizontal position, and dropping the legs at both knees, the person can keep air trapped in the boots (Fig. 163). The heavily clothed person can then float easily on front or back (Fig. 164) until determining whether to wait for assistance or carefully start to swim to safety.

If the fully clothed person wearing boots falls in feetfirst, air is usually forced out of the boots; however, enough air is trapped in the jacket to bring and keep the body up. The best position is a floating one, on the back, with the victim using gentle sculling or elementary backstroke arm action for easy propulsion and for maintaining position (Fig. 165). In both cases, additional air can be splashed into the jacket to add to buoyancy.

FIG. 163

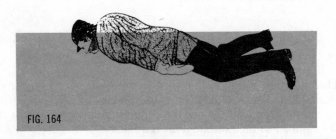

FIG. 164

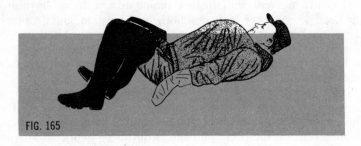

FIG. 165

EXPOSURE TO COLD WATER
(IMMERSION HYPOTHERMIA)

With the exception of immersion in waters warmer than 60°F, the main threat to life during prolonged immersion is cold or cold combined with the possibility of drowning.

An unclothed man of average body build will be helpless from hypothermia after from 20 to 30 minutes in water at 37°F and after about 1½ hours in water at 47°F. With thick conventional clothing, the times before hypothermia affects the victim increase to approximately 40 to 60 minutes in water at 37°F and to about 4 hours in water at 47°F (Fig. 166).

Unusual body builds cause great deviations from the above times. Thin persons become hypothermic more rapidly and fat persons less rapidly. Very fat persons may survive for long periods of time in water near 32°F if they are warmly clothed, although they cannot do so without clothing.

Immediately after a person enters cold water, it will be difficult to breathe normally. Float quietly in a flotation device or by clinging to a floating object, and the discomfort will rapidly decrease. If the person is not wearing a flotation device and there is no adequate floating object to cling to, the outer jacket should be inflated to provide a means of giving support with minimum activity.

A person who falls into cold water should not attempt to swim unless it is absolutely practical or necessary to do so—for example, if the person is being carried by current toward dangerous waters, such as waterfalls and dams, or if the distance to shore or safety is short. Even skilled swimmers are liable to drown suddenly if they attempt to swim any distance in very cold water, and few swimmers can cover as much as 200 yards in water near the freezing point. While floating and waiting for rescue in cold water, do not exercise in the water in an attempt to keep warm; exercising will actually have the reverse effect.

ESCAPE AND RESCUE FROM SUBMERGED VEHICLE

It is estimated that each year, over 400 persons lose their lives as a result of being trapped in automobiles that have plunged into water. In most cases, these fatalities are probably due to the fact that occupants try frantically to open the doors. They soon find that it is not immediately possible to do so; therefore, they panic and drown, trapped in the submerged vehicle.

Characteristics of the Submerged Vehicle

* Vehicles with all windows closed will float longer than those with all windows open, providing a greater chance of escape or rescue.
* Vehicles with engines in front will descend engine first at a steep angle. In water 15 feet deep or more, such a vehicle may rest on its top at the end of the descent.
* Doors cannot be opened until water pressure inside car is equal to that outside. When vehicle is completely filled, doors can be opened if there is no structural damage.
* Vehicles entering water at about 15 m.p.h. remain afloat for varying times. The more airtight the car, the longer it remains afloat.

Escape and Self-Rescue

* Wearing a safety belt will increase chances of occupants' surviving initial impact with water.
* Best escape technique from a vehicle floating on surface with wheels downward is through open windows before water reaches window level.
* If car sinks too rapidly for occupants to escape while vehicle is still on surface, they should move to rear of passenger compartment to breathe trapped air while planning escape. Then they can escape by (1) opening nearest window, (2) opening a door when water pressure inside is equal to outside pressure, or (3) pushing out rear window. Rear window is usually of tempered glass, which can be broken and disintegrated with a hammer, center punch, or similar strong, pointed object.
* Water rushing into vehicle through an open window at the moment window goes below surface makes escape through that window extremely difficult at that time. Occupants should wait until water in car is above upper level of window. This occurrence will be rapid.

Rescue From Outside Vehicle

* If car is floating on surface with all windows closed, the best way for rescuer to enter is through a window. Rear window probably will offer best opportunity. A hammer or center punch can be used to break tempered glass.
* Rescuers trying to enter vehicle through open windows should be aware of suction through windows while car is filling as windows disappear below surface.
* A rescuer taking an occupant from a station wagon with windows closed should first open tailgate if possible. Persons trapped

inside will probably have a better chance to escape if tailgate can be opened manually from inside.

Ways to escape from automobiles that have plunged into deep water have been listed by participants in a 1961 study at Williamston, Mich. The study was conducted by the Michigan State Police, the Indiana University Health and Safety Department, the Michigan Highway Department, and the American National Red Cross.

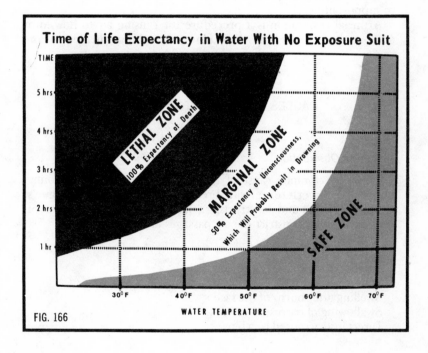

FIG. 166

11

RESPIRATORY EMERGENCIES AND ARTIFICIAL RESPIRATION

A respiratory emergency is one in which normal breathing stops or in which breathing is so reduced that oxygen intake is insufficient to support life.

Artificial respiration is a procedure for causing air to flow into and out of a person's lungs when natural breathing is inadequate or ceases.

CAUSES OF RESPIRATORY FAILURE

Anatomic Obstruction

The most common cause of respiratory emergency is anatomic obstruction, interference with breathing caused by the tongue's dropping back and obstructing the throat. Other causes of obstruction that constrict the air passages are—

Acute asthma
Croup
Diptheria
Spasm of the larynx
Swelling after burns of the face
Swallowing of corrosive poisons
Direct injury caused by a blow

Mechanical Obstruction

Partial or complete blockage of the air passage can be caused by a solid foreign object lodged in the pharnyx or in any part of the airway. Sudden death may occur from obstruction of the air passages directly or by pressure of a foreign body within the esophagus, which lies behind the trachea. In some instances of choking on food, a diagnosis of heart attack has been made on the basis of the victim's sudden collapse with marked chest pain, difficulty in breathing, and bluish discoloration of the face. A true life-threatening emergency exists only when a person is choking and having difficulty in breathing. If the victim is unable to speak, it is a sure indication that the larynx is completely obstructed.

Mechanical obstruction can also result from the accumulation of fluids in the back of the throat (mucus, blood, or saliva, for example), or from the inhalation of vomitus.

Air Depleted of Oxygen or Containing Toxic Gases

Asphyxia

Asphyxia may occur from breathing air that does not contain sufficient oxygen, or air containing carbon monoxide or other toxic gas. Natural, slow oxidation processes sometimes remove oxygen from the air in such places as wells, cisterns, sewers, mines, and silos.

If air does not contain oxygen, it will not support life, whether toxic gases are present or not. Plastic bags and other materials that may cause asphyxia when placed over the nose and mouth should be kept out of the reach of small children. Refrigerators and freezers, frequently the cause of accidents involving children, should never be abandoned unless the doors have been removed.

Explosion Hazard

In addition to the dangers of asphyxia from carbon monoxide, or from displacement of oxygen by natural oxidation processes or by other gases, there is often an explosion hazard. Combustible gases that accumulate in confined spaces—such as mines, cisterns, and sewers, or in rooms where natural or manufactured gas is free in the air—are explosive in certain concentrations. The explosion may result if a flame is introduced, if static electricity is discharged, or if an electric switch, doorbell, telephone, or other device is used.

Additional Causes

Additional causes of respiratory failure include—
- Electrocution
- Drowning
- Circulatory collapse (shock)
- Heart disease
- External strangulation, as in hanging
- Compression of the chest (caused, for example, by a mine cave-in)
- Disease or injury to the lungs

(Inadequate ventilation may be caused by injuries that collapse or compress lung tissue, injuries that permit air to enter through a sucking wound of the chest wall, accumulation of blood in the chest cavity from hemmorhage, or by inflammatory diseases of the lung such as pneumonia.)
• Poisoning by respiration-depressing drugs, such as morphine, opium, codeine, barbiturates, alcohol, and other narcotics.

THE BREATHING PROCESS

Contraction of chest muscles and diaphragm causes enlargement of the chest cavity. (The diaphragm is a muscular partition forming the floor of the chest cavity, separating the chest cavity from the abdomen.)

In the inhalation phase, the muscles of the chest lift the ribs, expanding the chest. The diaphragm, which is dome-shaped, contracts and descends toward the abdomen (Fig. 167A). In this way the chest cavity is increased in size, and atmospheric air flows in.

In the exhalation phase, the muscles relax, allowing the ribs and diaphragm to resume their former positions (Fig. 167B). The chest cavity becomes smaller, and air flows outward.

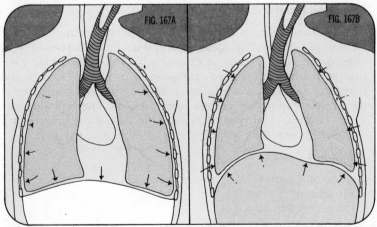

FIG. 167A   FIG. 167B

In adults at rest, the rate of breathing is from about 12 to 18 times per minute. The mouth-to-mouth or mouth-to-nose technique provides more ventilation by using direct air pressure exerted by the rescuer to inflate the victim's lungs immediately. It also enables the rescuer to obtain more accurate information on the volume, pressure, and timing of efforts needed to inflate the victim's lungs than is afforded by other methods. Another advantage of this method of artificial respiration, aside from its effectiveness in ventilating the lungs, is that it may be given in the water, in a boat, underneath wreckage, and in other places where immediate resuscitation might be necessary.

The manual methods of artificial respiration are chiefly of historical interest because they are not as effective as the mouth-to-mouth or mouth-to-nose method. The manual methods do not provide as much ventilation as the mouth-to-mouth or mouth-to-nose method, and it is not possible to maintain an open airway at all times when the manual methods are used.

When breathing movements have stopped and there is a lack of oxygen, the following signs and symptoms are usually seen:

- The victim's tongue, lips, and fingernails become blue.
- There is a loss of consciousness.
- The pupils of the eyes become dilated (enlarged).

ARTIFICIAL RESPIRATION

The objectives of artificial respiration are to maintain an open airway through the mouth and nose—or through the stoma (see page 189)—and to restore breathing by maintaining an alternating increase and decrease in the expansion of the chest.

The rate of breathing is somewhat faster in children and varies greatly with exercise, excitement, and disease. Approximately 1 pint of air is inhaled with each breath by resting adults, but not all of this air actually enters the lung tissue. For artificial respiration to be effective, the volume of air that enters must exceed the amount that is already in the air passages and that is needed for normal respiration. Hence, air should be forced into the victim.

The body does not store oxygen but needs a continuous, fresh supply to carry on the life processes. Oxygen must be available to all body cells and is transported throughout the body by the blood. Air entering the body is 21 percent oxygen and 0.04 percent carbon dioxide. The remainder is largely nitrogen. Air leaving the body is 16 percent oxygen and 4 percent carbon dioxide.

The mouth-to-mouth or mouth-to-nose technique of artificial respiration is the most practical method for emergency ventilation of a person of any age who has stopped breathing, regardless of why breathing has stopped. Extensive studies have indicated that mouth-to-mouth and mouth-to-nose resuscitation are clearly superior to any of the manual techniques.

The average person may die in 6 minutes or less if his oxygen supply is cut off. It is often impossible to tell exactly when a person has stopped breathing; he may be very near death when you first discover him. Therefore, artificial respiration always should be started as rapidly as possible. Recovery is usually rapid, except in cases of carbon monoxide poisoning, overdosage of drugs, or electrical shock. In these cases, it is often necessary to continue artificial respiration for a long time. When a victim revives, the person should be treated for shock. A physician's care is necessary during the recovery period.

Artificial respiration should always be continued until the victim begins to breathe for himself or is pronounced dead by a doctor or is dead beyond any doubt.

Mouth-to-Mouth (Mouth-to-Nose) Method

The mouth-to-mouth (mouth-to-nose) method of artificial respiration is carried out as follows:

1. Wipe any obvious foreign matter from the victim's mouth quickly (Fig. 168). Use your fingers, wrapped in a cloth if possible.

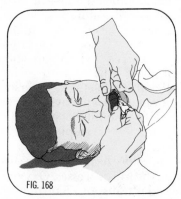

FIG. 168

2. The tongue of the unconscious victim in the supine position may drop back and block the throat (Fig. 169A). To open the air passage, place one hand beneath the victim's neck and lift. Place the heel of the other hand on the victim's forehead and rotate or tilt the head backward into maximum extension—the head-tilt method (Fig. 169B). Maintain the head in this position, since the position clears the airway by moving the tongue away from the back of the victim's throat. If additional

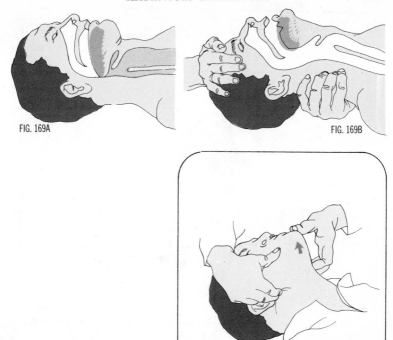

FIG. 169A

FIG. 169B

FIG. 169C

airway opening is required, it can be achieved by thrusting the lower jaw into a jutting-out position—the jaw-thrust method (Fig. 169C).

3. Pinch the victim's nostrils shut with the thumb and index finger of your hand that is pressing on the victim's forehead (Fig. 170A). This action prevents leakage of air when the lungs are inflated through the mouth. (Another way is to press your cheek against the victim's nose.)

4. Open your mouth widely, take a deep breath, seal your mouth tightly around the victim's mouth and, with your mouth forming a wide-open circle, blow into the mouth (Fig. 170B). Provide sufficient air. Volume is important. Start at a high rate and then provide at least one breath every 5 seconds for adults (or 12 per minute). If the airway is clear, only moderate resistance to blowing will be felt.

5. Watch the victim's chest to see when it rises. Stop blowing when the victim's chest is expanded. Raise your mouth, turn your head to the side, and listen for exhalation (Fig. 171).

6. Watch the chest to see that it falls.

7. Repeat the blowing cycle.

8. For the mouth-to-nose method, maintain the backward head-

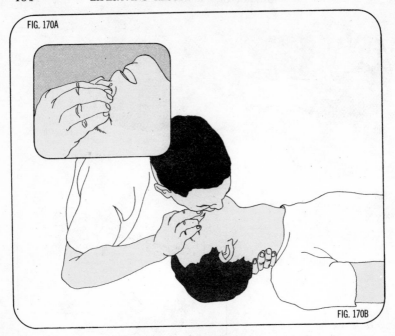

FIG. 170A

FIG. 170B

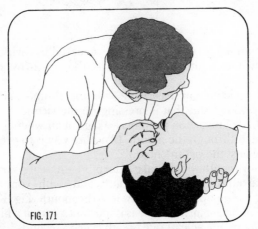

FIG. 171

tilt position with your hand on the victim's forehead. Use your other hand to close the victim's mouth (Fig. 172A). Open your mouth widely, take a deep breath, seal your mouth tightly around the victim's nose, and blow into the victim's nose (Fig. 172B). On the exhalation phase, open the victim's mouth to allow air to escape (Fig. 172C).

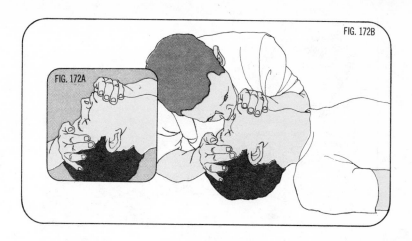

FIG. 172A

FIG. 172B

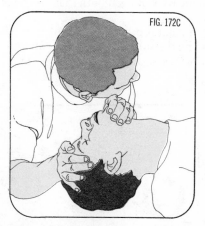

FIG. 172C

NOTE. Small children and infants are administered mouth-to-mouth or mouth-to-nose resuscitation as described above, except that the backward head tilt should not be as extensive as that for adults or large children. Both the mouth and nose of the infant or small child should be sealed off by your mouth (Fig. 173). Blow into the child's mouth and nose every 3 seconds (about 20 breaths per minute) with less pressure and volume than for an adult, the amount determined by the size of the child. Small puffs of air will suffice for infants.

FIG. 173

9. If you are not getting air exchange, recheck the position of the victim's head and jaw and check to see if there is foreign matter in the back of his mouth that may be obstructing the air passage.

10. If foreign matter is preventing ventilation, as a last resort, turn the victim on the side and administer sharp blows between the shoulder blades to jar the material free (Fig. 174).

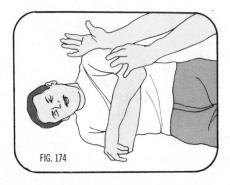

FIG. 174

A child may be suspended momentarily by the ankles or turned upside down over one arm and given two or three sharp pats between the shoulder blades (Fig. 175).

11. Clear the mouth again, reposition, and repeat the mouth-to-mouth or mouth-to-nose respiration.

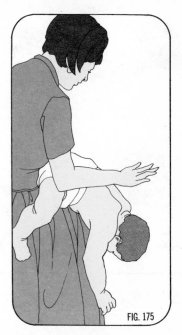

FIG. 175

12. If the victim's stomach is bulging, air may have been blown into the stomach, particularly when the air passage is obstructed or the inflation pressure is excessive. Although inflation of the stomach is not dangerous, it may make lung ventilation more difficult and increase the likelihood of vomiting.

13. If the victim's stomach is bulging, turn him face down for a moment, place both hands under the abdomen, and lift the abdomen to assist in emptying the stomach (Fig. 176A); otherwise, air in the stomach may interfere with both breathing and heart action. Another method is to leave the victim on the back, press on the stomach, and turn the head to the side (Fig. 176 B). These procedures will force air out of the stomach but may also cause regurgitation.

Some persons who require artificial respiration never stop breathing completely but gasp irregularly. The rescuer should not abandon mouth-to-mouth resuscitation until a normal pattern of respiration has been restored. The rescuer's blowing effort should be coordinated with the victim's inhalation.

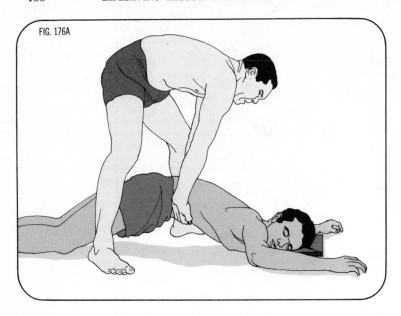

FIG. 176A

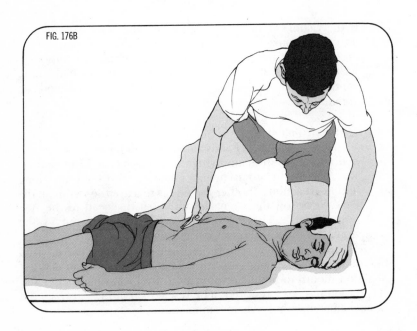

FIG. 176B

Mouth-to-Stoma Method

The Laryngectomee

In the United States there are about 25,000 persons whose larynxes have been completely or partially removed by surgery. The operation is called a *laryngectomy*. Those who have had the operation are called *laryngectomees* (Fig. 177).

A laryngectomee breathes through an opening called a *stoma* in the windpipe (trachea) in front of the neck. The individual cannot use nose or mouth for breathing.

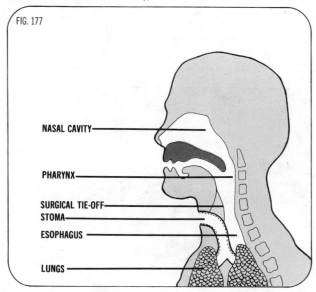

FIG. 177

NASAL CAVITY

PHARYNX

SURGICAL TIE-OFF

STOMA

ESOPHAGUS

LUNGS

First Aid for Laryngectomees

- When examining a victim of an accident or sudden illness, check the front of the neck to determine if the victim is a laryngectomee. (Most laryngectomees carry a card or other identification stating that they cannot breathe through the nose or mouth.)
- Do not inadvertently block the stoma when carrying out other first aid.

  The sound of escaping air, especially in combination with secretions or blood flow after injury in the neck area, may mislead the first-aider to conclude that the injury constitutes a sucking wound of the chest, and the first-aider may thus attempt to block the stoma with a pressure dressing. Blockage must be avoided, since it could cause death from asphyxiation.

- If a person is wearing a breathing tube in the stoma, it may be clogged, causing breathing difficulties. If the tube is clogged, remove it by lifting it out with the fingers. Removal of the tube will open the airway and will not cause immediate danger.

  If the laryngectomee is conscious, he may want to clean the tube and replace it himself, and he should be permitted to do so. Otherwise, the first-aider should send the tube with the victim to the hospital for replacement in the stoma.

- Give artificial respiration using the same general procedure as for mouth-to-mouth resuscitation, but place your mouth firmly over the victim's stoma. Blow at the same rate as for a person who breathes normally, watching the victim's chest for inflow of air (Fig. 178).

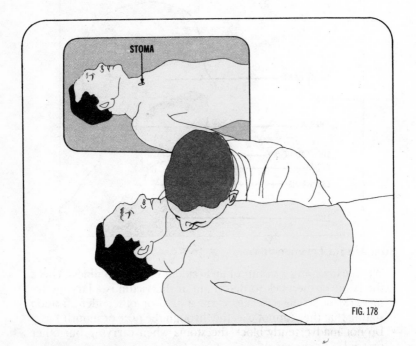

FIG. 178

Keep the victim's head straight. It is not necessary to tilt the head backward and to close off the victim's nose and mouth.

Avoid twisting the victim's head. Twisting might change the shape of, or close, the stoma.

The airway cannot be blocked by the victim's tongue or dentures.

Advantages of the Mouth-to-Stoma Method

The mouth-to-stoma method is more sanitary than mouth-to-mouth resuscitation because air coming from the stoma is cleaner than air coming from the mouth. Also, the contents of the laryngectomee's mouth cannot be vomited into the first-aider's mouth, because there is no connection between the stomach and the stoma.

The mouth-to-stoma method is preferred over a manual method since it is much more effective. The use of the chest pressure-arm lift method (Silvester method) is justified only when the only first-aider available is also a laryngectomee. If the manual method is used, make sure to keep the victim's head straight.

CARDIOPULMONARY RESUSCITATION (CPR)

Cardiopulmonary resuscitation (CPR) is the combination of artificial respiration and manual artificial circulation that is recommended for use in cases of cardiac arrest. It requires special training in the recognition of cardiac arrest and in the performance of CPR. Instruction includes manikin practice in performing both individually and as part of a team. Periodic retraining is required unless rescuers have repeated experiences in the application of CPR.

Cardiopulmonary resuscitation should be carried out only by qualified persons.

General Procedure

Cardiopulmonary resuscitation involves the following steps:
  A-Airway opening
  B-Breathing restored
  C-Circulation restored
  D-Definitive therapy
External cardiac compression consists of the application of rhythmic pressure over the lower half of the sternum. This pressure compresses the heart and produces a pulsatile artificial circulation. External cardiac compression must always be accompanied by artificial ventilation.

Definitive Therapy

Definitive therapy involves diagnosis, drugs, defibrillation (when indicated), and disposition. Definitive procedures are restricted to physicians or to members of allied health professions and author-

ized paramedical personnel under medical direction. The recom-
meded basic techniques for performing the *A* and *B* steps are
clearly defined in this text. The *C* and *D* steps are procedures
requiring special training. Red Cross chapters offer training in
cardiopulmonary resuscitation.

DROWNING, WATER ACCIDENTS, AND RESUSCITATION

Drowning is a type of asphyxia related to either aspiration of
fluids or obstruction of the airway caused by a spasm of the larynx.

Drowning is a major cause of accidental death in the United
States. It occurs in swimming, diving, boating, and other water
activities, including ice skating, and usually in unsupervised water
areas. Drownings can also occur in the home—in pools, bathtubs,
and washtubs—and in water that is only a few inches deep.

Causes of Drowning

Drowning may result from more than one cause. In some cases,
people die in the water from a heart attack, a stroke, or
overexertion. Fainting and epileptic attacks occur in water, just as
they do on land, and loss of consciousness itself may result in
accidental death. Occasionally, someone is struck by lightning while
swimming or wading. Drowning may follow a head injury sustained
in diving or in a collision with a log or other submerged object while
swimming.

Cramps in the muscles of the hand, foot, calf, thigh, or abdominal
wall may incapacitate a swimmer completely because of pain and
fright, and the victim may double over with the head submerged
and asphyxiate for lack of air. In cramping, muscles undergo
marked spasm when they suddenly contract. Relief is usually
obtained by stretching the involved muscles and applying firm
pressure from the time the first twinges of pain are felt until the
spasm is gone.

A drowning person may be seen either struggling in water and
making ineffectual movements, floating face down on the surface of
the water, or lying motionless underwater. Many persons sink very
quickly as they lose buoyancy by swallowing water and by aspirating
it into the lungs, where it replaces the tidal air (the volume of air
normally inhaled and exhaled). The victim sinks beneath the
surface and begins to lose consciousness from asphyxia. Effective
motion ceases, and the specific gravity of the victim's body becomes
greater than that of the water it displaces. Water pressure on the
victim's chest wall increases as the victim descends, forcing air out of

the lungs. The victim is unconscious but still may be revived if an attempt is made immediately.

Reflex Spasm of the Larynx

Asphyxia may occur from reflex spasm of the larynx, which closes the airway. This condition may occur immediately when the victim plunges into the water, especially if the water is cold, or as the result of pain, fear, or other conditions. Although the victim loses consciousness soon after slipping beneath the surface, the lungs may contain little or no water.

Submersion in Salt Water

If a person swallows and aspirates a large amount of sea water, the high concentration of salt will cause large amounts of fluid from the bloodstream to pass into and flood the lungs. Death may occur from shock, as a sudden fall in the blood pressure brings about circulatory collapse.

Submersion in Fresh Water

Fresh water sucked into a person's lungs enters the bloodstream and dilutes the blood. As the salt concentration of the blood lowers, red blood cells are destroyed.

Water may be absorbed so rapidly that the victim's lungs are relatively dry. More commonly, tremendous swelling takes place, and frothy, pink-tinged fluid accumulates in the lungs as a result of ruptured red blood cells.

Adequate ventilation of the lungs after rescue may be impossible because of water blockage. Death may occur from either asphyxia or heart failure.

Performing Artificial Respiration in the Water

If it is necessary to give artificial respiration in the water, the rescuer should begin mouth-to-mouth respiration as quickly as possible in shallow water or while holding onto a boat, the side of a pool (Figs. 179 and 180), or a suitable buoyant aid. The rescuer must be alert to the possibility of an obstruction in the air passages and must act immediately if one occurs.

- Blow into the victim's mouth or nose more forcefully than in other types of emergencies affecting respiration, to force air through water or other obstruction in the air passage.
- After inflating the victim's lungs with 10 quick breaths, move to shore or pull the victim onto a suitable flotation device unless there is evidence of an injury to the spinal cord in the neck or

FIG. 179

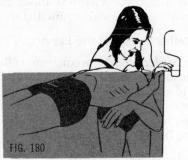

FIG. 180

back, which requires a backboard or other rigid support (see pages 209 through 214).

In deep water, adequate inflation can be provided by trained rescuers if a flotation device is provided and can be placed under the victim's neck. This device provides a support that keeps the victim's mouth and nose out of the water and allows the rescuer to inflate the lungs without water getting into the air passages.

In deep water, it is usually impossible even for trained rescuers to provide adequate volume and rate of lung inflation when there is no flotation device available. Attempts at mouth-to-mouth and mouth-to-nose resuscitation under these circumstances are ill advised, and the rescuer should attempt to get the victim into shallow water or close to some object in the water with which the rescuer can support himself and begin artificial respiration. Such support is especially important in instances where the rescuer is not a strong swimmer, or is not highly trained in deep-water rescue, or where rough water renders rescue efforts difficult.

If a strong swimmer who is well trained in deep-water rescue feels that he can get one or two good breaths into a victim before starting for shore, he can attempt to do so. However, valuable time should not be lost with continued unsuccessful attempts at ventilation. An ordinary swimmer should not attempt this maneuver.

Supplemental Care of Victim

Immediately after rescue, the rescuer should begin artificial respiration, treat for shock, and transport the victim to a place where medical care can be received. Water-accident victims who die usually do so within 10 minutes after the accident, from lack of air or from heart failure, not directly because of the presence of water in the lungs or the stomach. It is not possible to remove water out of the lungs, and no attempt should be made to do so.

A victim who has been successfully revived from a near-drowning accident should not be allowed to walk. Because delayed complications, such as pneumonia, may develop, the victim should receive immediate medical attention and should be closely watched for several days, preferably in a hospital. Deaths that could have been prevented have occurred more than 48 hours after initial resuscitation.

12

EMERGENCY FIRST AID

The first aid advice contained in this chapter relates to life-threatening and other injuries or conditions that might occur in the aquatic environment and is based on the current edition of the Red Cross first aid textbooks. Additional first aid knowledge and skills that can save life and prevent unnecessary suffering are given in American Red Cross first aid courses.

Proper knowledge and skill in first aid are a must for every person. They are particularly necessary for those individuals who are responsible for the safety of others who are in, on, or about the water. The application of first aid knowledge and skill often means the difference between temporary and permanent disability and the difference between rapid recovery and long hospitalization.

First aid training is of value in—
- Teaching prevention and care in accidental injury or sudden illness
- Training people to care for those caught in natural disaster or other catastrophe
- Equipping individuals to deal with the whole situation, the person, and the injury
- Helping the first-aider to distinguish between what to do and what not to do

The limitation of time in case of an accident or sudden illness may be so critical in terms of minutes or even seconds that only a person with first aid knowledge and skills who is on hand has any opportunity to prevent a fatal outcome. The first aid trained individual may encounter a variety of problem situations. The first-aider's decisions and actions will vary according to the circumstances that produced the accident or sudden illness and according to the number of persons involved, the immediate environment, the availability of medical assistance, emergency dressings and equipment, and help from others. The first-aider will need to adapt what he or she has learned to the situation at hand, or to improvise. Sometimes, prompt action is needed to save a life. At other times, there is no need for haste, and efforts will be directed toward preventing further injury, obtaining assistance, and reassuring the victim, who may be emotionally upset and apprehensive as well as in pain.

GENERAL DIRECTIONS FOR GIVING FIRST AID

In case of serious injury or sudden illness, while help is being summoned, the first-aider should give *immediate* attention to the following first aid priorities:
- Effect a prompt rescue.
- Make sure that the victim has an open airway and give mouth-to-mouth or mouth-to-nose artificial respiration, if necessary.
- Control severe bleeding.
- Give first aid for poisoning or ingestion of harmful chemicals.

Once emergency measures have been taken to insure the victim's safety, the following procedures should be carried out:
- Do *not* move a victim unless it is necessary for safety reasons.

Keep the victim in the position best suited to the individual's condition or injuries; do not let the victim get up or walk about.
- Protect the victim from unnecessary manipulation and disturbance.
- Avoid or overcome chilling by using blankets or covers, if available.

If exposure to cold or dampness is likely, place blankets or additional clothing over and under the victim.
- Determine the injuries or cause for sudden illness. After immediate problems are under control—
  1. Find out exactly what happened. Information may be obtained from the victim or from persons who were present and saw the accident, or saw the individual collapse in the case of sudden illness.
  2. Look for an emergency medical identification, such as a card or bracelet, which may provide a clue to the victim's condition.
  3. If the victim is unconscious and has *no* sign of external injury, and if the above methods fail to provide identity, try to obtain proper identification either from papers carried in the victim's billfold or purse or from bystanders, so that relatives may be notifed. (It is advisable to have a witness when searching for identification.)
- Examine the victim methodically but be guided by the kind of accident or sudden illness and the needs of the situation. Have a reason for what you do. In general, proceed as follows:

1. Loosen constricting clothing but do not pull on the victim's belt in case spinal injuries are present.
2. Open or remove clothing if necessary to expose a body part in order to make a more accurate check for injuries. Clothing may be cut away or ripped at the seams, but utmost caution must be used, or added injury may result. Do not expose the victim unduly without protective cover, and use discretion if clothing must be removed.
3. Note the victim's general appearance, including skin discolloration, and check all symptoms that may give a clue to the injury or sudden illness.

   In the case of a victim with dark skin, change in skin color may be difficult to note. It may then be necessary to depend upon change in the color of the mucous membrane, or inner surface of the lips, mouth, and eyelids.
4. Check the victim's pulse. If you cannot feel it at the wrist, check for a pulse of the carotid artery at the side of the neck.
5. Check to see if the victim is awake, stuporous, or unconscious. Does the victim respond to questions?
6. If the victim is unconscious, look for evidence of head injury. In a conscious person, look for paralysis of one side of the face or body. See if the victim shows evidence of a recent convulsion. (The tongue may have been bitten, producing a laceration.)
7. Check the expression of the victim's eyes and the size of the pupils.
8. Examine the victim's trunk and limbs for open and closed wounds or for signs of fractures.
9. Check the front of the victim's neck to determine whether the individual is a laryngectomee (see Mouth-to-Stoma Method, page 189). Most laryngectomees carry a card or other identification stating that they cannot breathe through the nose or mouth.

   Do not block the stoma (air inlet) of a laryngectomee when carrying out other first aid, since blockage could cause death from asphyxiation.
10. If poisoning is suspected, check for stains or burns about the victim's mouth and a source of poisoning nearby, such as pills, medicine bottles, household chemicals, or pesticides.

- Carry out the indicated first aid:
  1. Apply emergency dressings, bandages, and splints, as indicated.
  2. Do not move the victim unless absolutely necessary.
  3. Plan action according to the nature of the accident or sudden

illness, the needs of the situation, and the availability of human and material resources.

4. Utilize proper first aid measures and specific techniques that, under the circumstances, appear to be reasonably necessary.

5. Remain in charge until the victim can be turned over to qualified persons (for example, a physician, an ambulance crew, a rescue squad, or a police officer), or until the victim can take care of himself or can be placed in care of relatives.

6. Do not attempt to make a diagnosis of any sort or to discuss a victim's condition with bystanders or reporters.

7. Above all, as a first aid worker, you should know the limits of your capabilities and must make every effort to avoid further injury to the victim in your attempt to provide the best possible emergency first aid care.

FIRST AID FOR SEVERE BLEEDING

When blood is spurting or gushing from a wound, it must be controlled immediately, or death will result within a few minutes.

Direct Pressure and Elevation ·

Direct pressure by hand over a dressing is the preferred method for the control of severe bleeding (Fig. 181). In an emergency, in

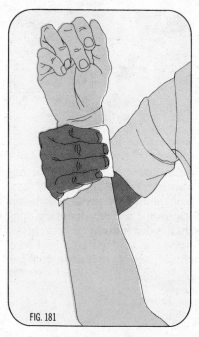

FIG. 181

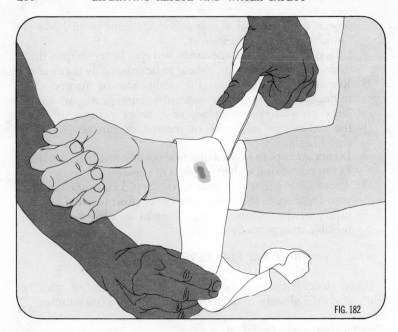

FIG. 182

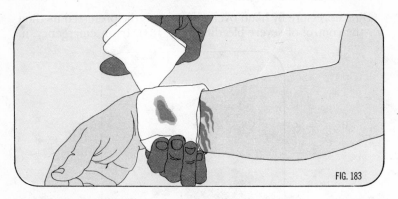

FIG. 183

the absence of compresses, the bare hand or fingers may be used, but only until a compress can be applied.

On most parts of the body, a pressure bandage can be placed to hold pads of cloth over a severely bleeding open wound and free the hands of the first-aider for other emergency action (Fig. 182).

Also elevate (raise the affected part to a level higher than the heart) if there are no fractures or if additional pain or harm will not be inflicted.

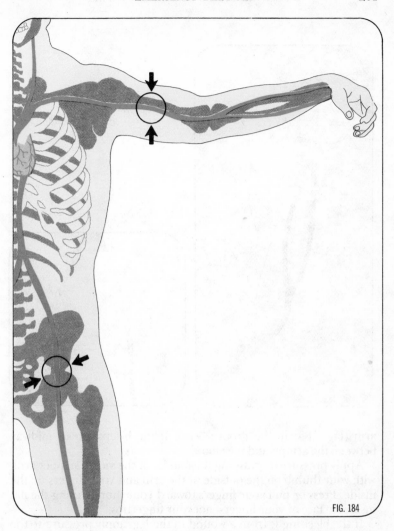

FIG. 184

If blood soaks through the entire pad without clotting, do not remove the pad but add additional layers (Fig. 183). Do not disturb blood clots after they have formed within the cloth.

If direct pressure does not control the bleeding, apply pressure at the appropriate pressure point while maintaining pressure over the wound as well as continuing elevation (Fig. 184).

If the bleeding is from a wound in the arm, apply pressure to the brachial artery. This pressure point is located on the inside of the

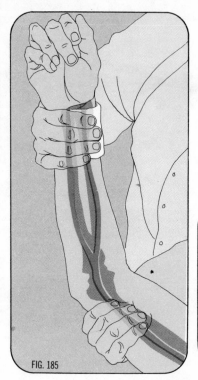

FIG. 185

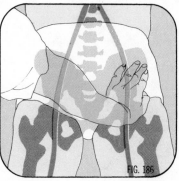

FIG. 186

arm (Fig. 185) in the groove between the biceps, about midway between the armpit and the elbow.

Apply pressure by grasping the middle of the victim's upper arm, with your thumb on the outside of the arm and your fingers on the inside. Press or pull your fingers toward your thumb, using the flat inside surface of your fingers, not your fingertips.

If the bleeding is from a wound in the leg, apply pressure to the femoral artery. This pressure point is located on the front center part of the diagonally slanted "hinge" of the leg, in the crease of the groin area and over the pelvic bone.

Apply pressure by placing the heel of your hand directly over the spot described above (Fig. 186). Lean forward with your arm straightened to apply the pressure.

It is important when using the pressure points (brachial or femoral arteries) that you maintain pressure over the wound as well as elevation.

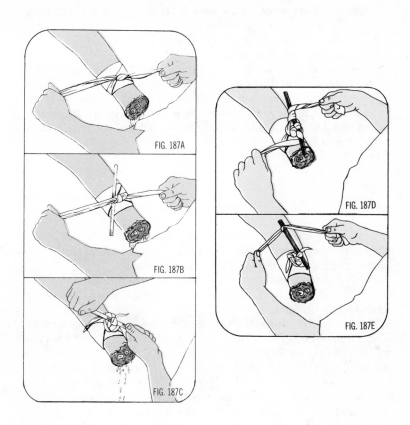

FIG. 187A

FIG. 187B

FIG. 187C

FIG. 187D

FIG. 187E

Tourniquet

If the above methods do not control severe bleeding and the victim is in danger of bleeding to death, the tourniquet may be used as a *last resort* to save life.

The tourniquet should be used only for the severe life-threatening hemorrhage that cannot be controlled by other means. This method is used only on the arm or leg. Once a tourniquet is applied, care by a physician is imperative.

To apply the tourniquet—

1. Place the tourniquet just above the wound, but not touching the wound edges (Fig. 187A). If the wound is in a joint area or just below, place the tourniquet directly above the joint.
2. Wrap the tourniquet band tightly twice around the limb and tie a half knot.

3. Place a short, strong stick (or similar object) on the half knot and tie a full knot (Fig. 187B).
4. Twist the stick until bleeding is stopped (Fig. 187C).
5. Secure the stick in place (Figs. 187D and 187E).
6. Attach a note to the victim giving the location of the tourniquet and the time that it was applied.
7. *Once the serious decision to apply the tourniquet has been made, the tourniquet should not be loosened except on the advice of a physician.*
8. Treat for shock and get medical attention for the victim immediately.

Do not cover a tourniquet.

SHOCK

Shock is a condition resulting in a depressed state of many vital body functions, a depression that could threaten life even though the victim's injuries would not otherwise be fatal.

Injury-related shock, commonly referred to as traumatic shock, is decidedly different from electrical shock, insulin shock, and other special forms of shock.

Shock may be caused by severe injuries of all types—hemorrhage; loss of body fluids other than blood (as in prolonged vomiting, dysentery, or burns); infection; heart attack or stroke; or poisoning by chemicals, gases, alcohol, or drugs. Shock also results from lack of oxygen caused by obstruction of air passages. The degree of shock is increased by abnormal changes in body temperature and by poor resistance of the victim to stress. Shock is aggravated by pain, by rough handling, and by delay in treatment.

Signs and Symptoms

In the early stages of shock, the body compensates for a decreased blood flow to the tissues by constricting the blood vessels in the skin, in the organs of the abdominal cavity, and in the skeletal muscles. The following signs may develop as a result:

- The skin is pale (or bluish) and cold to the touch. In the care of victims with dark skin, it may be necessary to rely primarily on the color of the mucous membranes on the inside of the mouth or under the eyelids, or on the color of the nail beds.
- The skin may be moist and clammy if perspiration has occurred.
- The victim is weak.
- The pulse is usually quite rapid (over 100) and often too faint to be felt at the wrist (Fig. 188A) but perceptible in the carotid

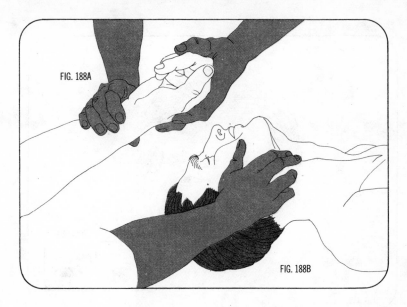

FIG. 188A

FIG. 188B

artery (Fig. 188B) at the side of the neck or in the femoral artery at the groin.
- The rate of breathing is usually increased; it may be shallow, possibly deep and irregular.
- If there has been injury to the chest or abdomen, breathing will almost certainly be shallow, because of the pain involved in breathing deeply.
- A victim in shock from hemorrhage may be restless and anxious (early signs of oxygen lack), thrashing about, and complaining of severe thirst.
- The victim may vomit or retch from nausea.
If the victim's condition deteriorates, the following additional signs may be noted:
- The victim becomes apathetic and relatively unresponsive.
- The victim's eyes are sunken, with a vacant expression, and the pupils may be widely dilated (Fig. 189).
- Some of the blood vessels in the skin may be dilated, producing a mottled appearance, which indicates the victim's blood pressure has fallen to a very low level.
- If untreated, the victim eventually loses consciousness, the body temperature falls, and the person may die.

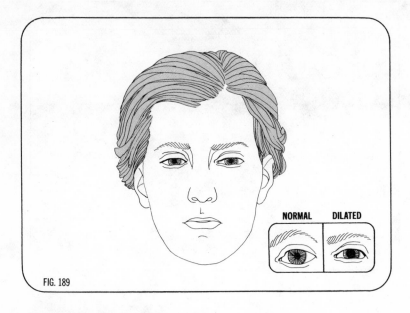

NORMAL   DILATED

FIG. 189

Objectives of First Aid Care

Objectives are to improve circulation of the blood, to ensure an adequate supply of oxygen, and to maintain normal body temperature.

First Aid

Give urgently necessary first aid immediately to help prevent or to control the causes of shock, such as stoppage of breathing, hemorrhaging, or severe pain.

Steps for preventing shock and for giving first aid are as follows:

1. Keep the victim lying down.
2. Cover the victim *only* enough to keep him from losing body heat.
3. Get medical help as soon as possible.

The body position for a victim must be based on his injuries. Generally, the most satisfactory position for the injured person will be lying down to improve the circulation of blood.

If injuries of the neck or lower spine are suspected, *do not* move the victim until the person is properly prepared for transportation, unless it is necessary to protect the victim from further injury or to provide urgent first aid care.

A victim with severe wounds of the lower part of the face and jaw, or who is unconscious, should be placed on the side to allow drainage of fluids and to avoid blockage of the airway by vomitus and blood (Fig. 190). Extreme care must be taken to ensure an open airway and to prevent asphyxia. When there is no danger of aspiration of fluids, a victim who is having difficulty breathing may be placed on the back with the head and shoulders raised (Fig. 191).

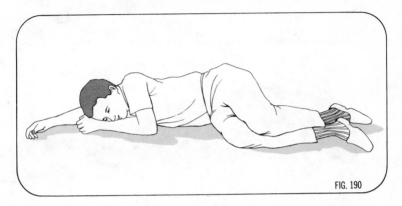

FIG. 190

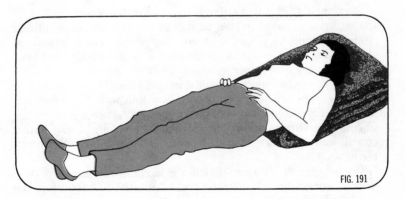

FIG. 191

A person with a head injury may be kept flat or propped up, but the head must not be lower than the rest of the body.

If in doubt concerning the proper position of the victim based on injuries sustained, keep the person lying flat.

Victims in shock may improve if the feet (or foot of the stretcher) are raised from 8 to 12 inches (Fig. 192). If the victim has increased difficulty in breathing or experiences additional pain after the feet are raised, lower the feet again.

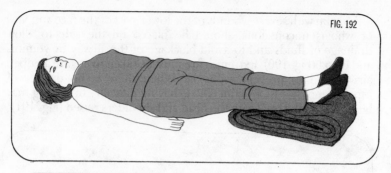

FIG. 192

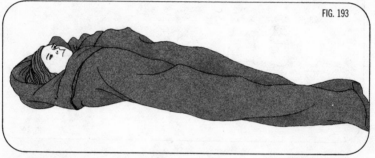

FIG. 193

Keep the victim warm enough to avoid or overcome chilling. If the victim is exposed to cold or dampness, blankets or additional clothing should be placed over and under the person to prevent chilling (Fig. 193). No attempt should be made to add extra heat, because raising the surface temperature of the body is harmful.

Giving fluids by mouth has value in shock, but fluids should only be given when medical help is not available within a reasonable time. Fluids should not be given, however, when victims are unconscious, are vomiting or are likely to vomit, or are having convulsions, since victims in such conditions may aspirate fluids into the lungs.

Do not give fluids when a victim is likely to require surgery or general anesthetic, or when the person appears to have a brain or abdominal injury.

Fluids may be given by mouth only if medical care is delayed for an hour or more and no contraindications exist. Water that is neither hot nor cold—preferably a salt-soda solution (containing 1 level teaspoonful of salt and ½ level teaspoonful of baking soda to each quart of water) should be given as follows:
• Give an adult victim about 4 ounces (½ glass) every 15 minutes.
• Give approximately 2 ounces to children aged from 1 to 12, and 1 ounce to infants of 1 year or less.

- Discontinue fluids if the victim becomes nauseated or vomits.
- From 2 to 4 hours later, resume normal fluid intake according to the victim's tolerance.

SPINAL INJURIES

Description and Characteristics

The backbone, or spinal column, is composed of 33 bones called vertebrae, which enclose the spinal cord. If a vertebra, or one of the disks that separate the vertebrae, is fractured or dislocated, the spinal cord may be injured, and loss of motion and sensation below the level of injury may result. Diving is a common cause of this kind of injury. Injury to the spinal cord should be suspected if the injured person is unable to move either the arms or legs after an accident or if the person complains of numbness or pain.

For fracture or dislocation in the neck region, there is usually severe pain, spasm of the neck muscles, and difficulty in moving the head. There will be weakness and numbness below the level of injury if the injury is slight, or paralysis and loss of sensation when damage is serious. Symptoms of fracture of the trunk region (upper and lower back) are similar to those associated with the neck injury. There is pain at the affected site, which extends around the chest or abdomen or down the legs, along the course of the spinal nerves. There is also tenderness over the injury, muscle spasm, and weakness or paralysis and disturbance of sensation below the level of injury.

If a spinal injury is suspected, extreme care should be taken to avoid any twisting, bending, or side-to-side motion of the victim's head and trunk. After rescue in a water accident, the victim should be kept floating in shallow water until an ambulance with trained personnel can be obtained. Needless to say, proper first aid must be given for other life-threatening injuries, such as stoppage of breathing or hemorrhage from an open wound. Keep the victim floating, with one hand supporting the shoulders and head while the other hand keeps the head immobile.

If removal from the water is absolutely necessary before trained personnel arrive—
- Have adequate help (three or four persons).
- Make sure that all concerned clearly understand the best method of keeping the body as rigid as possible without subjecting the body to twisting, bending, or side-to-side motion.
- Preferably, practice briefly on an uninjured person before attempting to move the victim.

The basic procedure involved in removing a victim with a suspected spinal injury from the water includes the following actions:

1. Give necessary first aid, such as artificial respiration, control of bleeding, and, possibly, splinting.
2. Use a spine board, or if one is not available, a rigid support such as a door, surfboard, aquaplane, or ironing board.
3. Place the board under the victim by sliding it under the water and letting it float up.
4. Once the board is in place, as an additional precaution to protect the victim from sliding or rolling, use any available material to secure the victim's body to the rigid support.
5. Take extreme care to avoid any unnecessary movement that might subject the victim's body to twisting, bending, or side-to-side motion.

Neck and Spine Injuries in Water Accidents

Injuries resulting from water accidents require special first aid measures because of the frequent occurrence of cervical fractures, complicated by the possibility of drowning. Because cervical spine injuries are more likely to result in severing of the spinal cord than other vertebral fractures, protection against paralysis from spinal cord damage is imperative. Whenever possible, a trained assistant should be summoned and requested to bring a backboard, and the victim *should not* be removed from the water until the backboard arrives. If a backboard is not available, any rigid support may be adaptable, such as a wooden door, a surfboard, an aquaplane, a wooden plank, an ironing board, a picnic table bench, a water ski, or any similar item that will not break or bend.

If the victim is floating face down, turn him over carefully with the least amount of movement, keeping his head and body aligned. Place one of your hands in the middle of the victim's back with your arm right over his head; place your other hand under the victim's upper arm, close to the shoulder (Fig. 194), ready to turn him to the face-up position. Rotate the victim by lifting his shoulder up and over with one hand while your other hand and arm support and maintain his head and body alignment (Figs. 195 and 196).

The same technique of turning a victim over must be used even if the victim is found floating in deep water. If a rigid back support is readily available, a helper should bring it out and slide it under the victim, and the victim, supported by the board, can be carefully moved to standing-depth water before the tie-down bandages are applied. The original rescuer maintains hand support at the head while the helper can provide propulsion at the lower end of the

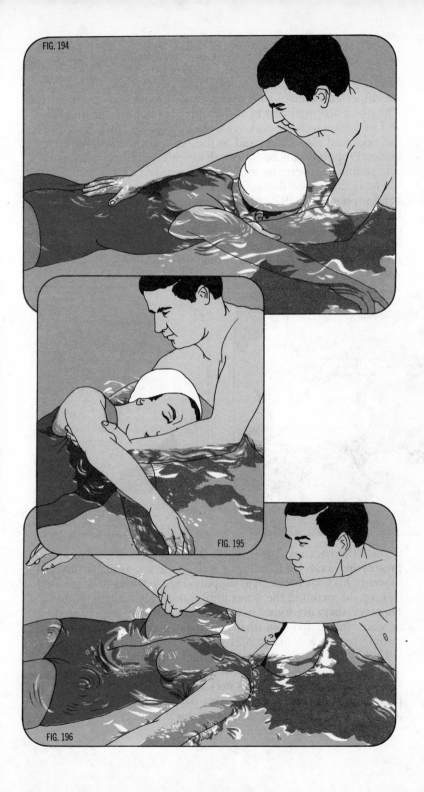

FIG. 194

FIG. 195

FIG. 196

board. When no support is quickly available, the rescuer must tow the suspected victim of such a back injury to standing-depth water. The tow is accomplished by the rescuer, keeping the victim's head and neck level with the back, with one hand supporting the back of the neck and the other hand at the back, between the shoulder blades. Propulsion will be entirely done with the rescuer's leg action, using either an inverted scissors or breaststroke kick.

The victim can be floated on his back in the water with minimal hand support (Fig. 197). Always keep his head and neck level with his back, and keep his airway open. If mouth-to-mouth resuscitation must be administered, use the jaw-thrust maneuver without head tilt (Fig. 198). Place the backboard under the victim by sliding it under the water and letting it float up (Fig. 199).

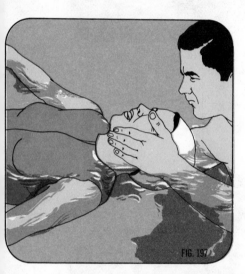

FIG. 197

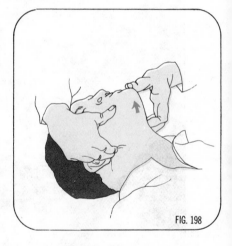

FIG. 198

Once the backboard is in place, as an additional precaution to protect the victim from sliding or rolling, use any available material to secure his body to the rigid support (Figs. 200 and 201). It is best to keep the victim in the water until trained assistance is available. However, there are some circumstances, such as excessive bleeding or water that is too cold, that may make it urgent to remove the victim from the water (Fig. 202).

Under such conditions, if no rigid support of any kind is available, constantly bear in mind the possibility of a cervical fracture and keep the victim's neck as nearly level with his back as possible by placing the heels of your palms at the back of his head and extending your fingers down onto his shoulders.

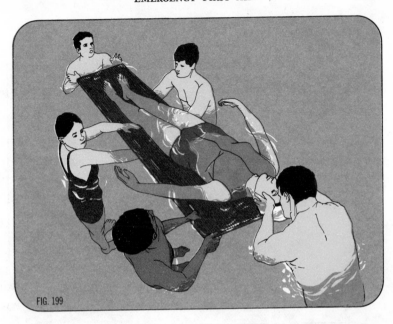

FIG. 199

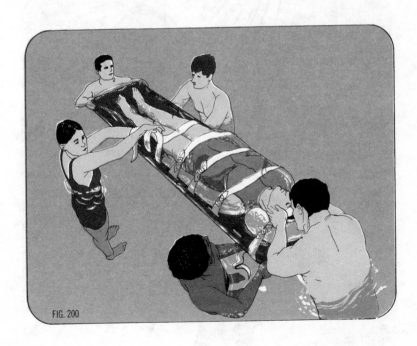

FIG. 200

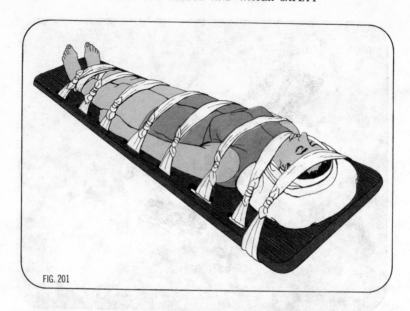

FIG. 201

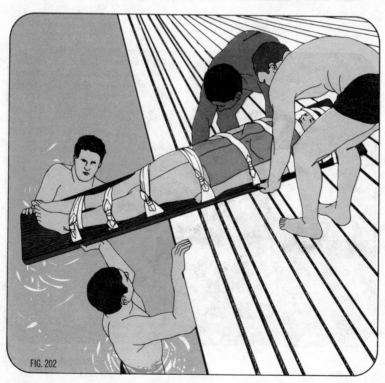

FIG. 202

BURNS

A burn is an injury that results from heat, chemical agents, or radiation. It may vary in depth, size, and severity, causing injury to the cells in the affected areas.

Classification

Burns are usually classified according to depth or degree of skin damage. Often the degree will differ in various parts of the same affected area.

First-degree burns (Fig. 203) are those resulting from overexposure to the sun, light contact with hot objects, or scalding by hot water or steam. The usual signs are redness or discoloration, mild swelling, and pain. Healing occurs rapidly. NOTE: Severe sunburn should receive medical care as soon as possible.

Second-degree burns (Fig. 204) are those resulting from a very deep sunburn, contact with hot liquids, and flash burns from gasoline, kerosene, and other products. Second-degree burns are usually more painful than deeper burns in which the nerve endings in the skin are destroyed. The usual signs are greater depth than

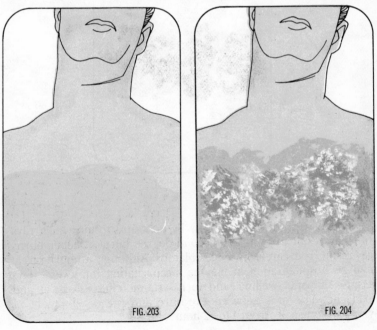

FIG. 203   FIG. 204

first-degree burns, red or mottled appearance, development of blisters, considerable swelling over a period of several days, and wet appearance of the surface of the skin due to the loss of plasma through the damaged layers of the skin.

Third-degree burns (Fig. 205) can be caused by a flame, ignited clothing, immersion in hot water, contact with hot objects, or electricity. Temperature and duration of contact are important factors in determining the extent of tissue destruction. The usual signs are deep tissue destruction, white or charred appearance (at first, possibly resembling a second-degree burn), and complete loss of all layers of the skin.

FIG. 205

Sunburn

Sunburn is produced primarily by exposure to ultraviolet rays and may result in first- and second-degree burns. Deeper burns may result from careless use of sunlamps. Although sunburn rarely requires hospitalization, it may be incapacitating for several days because of pain, swelling, and such systemic effects as fever and headache. The time between exposure and the development of symptoms is usually from 4 to 12 hours.

First aid for sunburn is the same as for first- and second-degree burns. If later medical treatment appears likely, do not apply ointment to the sunburn. Any person with extensive sunburn (10 percent or more of the body surface in a child and 15 percent or more in an adult) should be seen by a physician. Likewise, very deep burns with many large blisters should have medical treatment. If blisters break, apply a dry, sterile dressing.

First Aid

The objective of first aid for burns is to relieve pain, prevent contamination, and treat for shock. The following chart gives the first aid advice for burns according to classification.

Burn	Do	Don't
First degree (redness, mild swelling, and pain)	• Use running tap water or cold water application. • Apply dry, sterile dressing. • Use addidional home remedies as advised by physician.	• Apply butter, oleomargarine, etc.
Second degree (deeper than first degree, with blisters developing)	• Immerse in cold water. • Blot dry with sterile cloth. • Apply dry, sterile cloth for protection. • Treat patient for shock. • Obtain medical attention if severe.	• Break blisters. • Remove shreds of tissue. • Use antiseptic preparation, ointment, spray, or home remedy on severe burn.
Third degree (deeper destruction, with skin layers destroyed)	• Cover with sterile cloth to protect. • Treat patient for shock. • Watch for breathing difficulty. • Obtain medical attention quickly.	• Remove charred clothing that is stuck to burn. • Apply ice. • Use home medication.
Chemical burn	• Remove by flushing with large quantities of water for at least 5 minutes. • After flushing eye, apply sterile pad for protection. • Obtain medical attention.	

HEAT STROKE, HEAT CRAMPS,
AND HEAT EXHAUSTION

Excessive heat may affect the body in a variety of ways, which result in several conditions referred to as heat stroke, heat cramps, and heat exhaustion.

Definitions

- Heat stroke is a response to heat characterized by extremely high body temperature and disturbance of the sweating mechanism. Heat stroke is an immediate, life-threatening emergency, for which medical care is urgently needed.
- Heat cramps involve muscular pains and spasms due largely to loss of salt from the body in sweating or to inadequate intake of salt. Heat cramps may be associated, also, with heat exhaustion.
- Heat exhaustion is a response to heat characterized by fatigue, weakness, and collapse due to intake of water inadequate to compensate for loss of fluids through sweating.

Causes

Heat reactions are brought about by both internal and external factors. Harmful effects occur when the body becomes overheated and cannot eliminate the excess heat. Reactions usually occur when large amounts of water, salt, or both are lost through profuse sweating following strenuous exercise or manual labor in an extremely hot atmosphere. Elderly individuals, small children, chronic invalids, alcoholics, and overweight persons are particularly susceptible to heat reactions, especially during heat waves in areas where a moderate climate usually prevails.

Signs, Symptoms, and First Aid

Heat Stroke

Signs and Symptoms
- Body temperature is high (may be 106°F or higher).
- Skin is characteristically hot, red, and dry (Fig. 206), since the sweating mechanism is blocked.
- Pulse is rapid and strong.
- Victim may be unconscious.

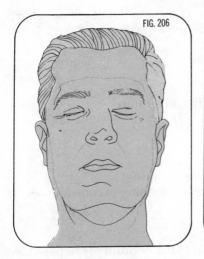

FIG. 206

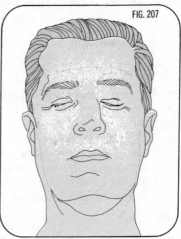

FIG. 207

First Aid
- First aid should be directed toward immediate measures to cool the body quickly. Take care, however, to prevent overchilling of victim once the body temperature is reduced below 102°F.

The following first aid measures are applicable whenever the body temperature reaches 105°F:
- Undress victim and, using a bath towel to maintain modesty, repeatedly sponge the bare skin with cool water or rubbing alcohol; or apply cold packs continuously; or place victim in a tub of cold water (do not add ice) until the person's temperature is lowered sufficiently.
- When the temperature has been reduced enough, dry victim off.
- Use fans or air conditioners, if available, because drafts will promote cooling.
- If victim's temperature starts to go up again, start the cooling process again.
- Do not give victim stimulants.

Heat Cramps

Symptoms
- In the case of heat cramps, the muscles of legs and abdomen are likely to be affected first.

First Aid
- Exert firm pressure with your hands on cramped muscles, or gently massage them, to help relieve the spasm.

- Give victim sips of salt water (1 teaspoonful of salt per glass), half a glass every 15 minutes, over a period of about 1 hour.

Heat Exhaustion

Symptoms

- Approximately normal body temperature
- Pale and clammy skin (Fig. 207)
- Profuse perspiration
- Tiredness, weakness
- Headache and perhaps cramps
- Nausea and dizziness (possible vomiting)
- Possible fainting (but probable regaining of consciousness as victim's head is lowered)

First Aid

- Give victim sips of salt water (1 teaspoonful of salt per glass, every 15 minutes), over a period of about 1 hour.
- Have victim lie down and raise the feet from 8 to 12 inches.
- Loosen victim's clothing.
- Apply cool, wet cloths and fan victim or remove the individual to an air-conditioned room.
- If victim vomits, do not give any more fluids. Take victim as soon as possible to a hospital, where an intravenous salt solution can be given.
- After an attack of heat exhaustion, the victim should rest and should be protected from further exposure to abnormally warm temperatures. It may be advisable for the victim to seek medical guidance before engaging in hard labor or physical exertion.

SUDDEN ILLNESS

First aid workers often encounter emergencies that are not related to injury but arise from either sudden illness or a crisis in a chronic illness. Unless the illness is minor and brief, such as a fainting attack, airsickness, a nosebleed, or a headache, medical assistance should be sought. Although sudden illness is not always urgent, sometimes it endangers a person's life, especially if associated with a heart attack or a massive internal hemorrhage. An important first aid measure in such an instance is to secure transportation of the victim to medical care as quickly as possible.

Many persons suffering from heart disease, stroke, epilepsy, or diabetes carry an identification card or bracelet that contains information about the type of illness and steps to be followed if the persons are found unconscious. Search the victim (in the presence of witnesses) for such identification.

Heart Attack

Heart attack usually involves a clot in one of the blood vessels that supply the heart. The attack is sometimes called a coronary, since there is a loss of blood supply to a portion of the heart muscle. A heart attack may or may not be accompanied by loss of consciousness. If the attack is severe, the victim may die suddenly. The victim may have a history of heart disease, or the attack may come with little or no warning. Attacks with mild pain sometimes occur. The degree of pain is not a good indication of the seriousness of the attack.

Signs and Symptoms

Signs and symptoms of heart attack include—
- Persistent chest pain, usually under the sternum (breastbone), but sometimes affecting both the sternum area and the left shoulder and arm
- Gasping and shortness of breath
- Extreme pallor or bluish discoloration of the lips, skin, and fingernails
- Extreme prostration
- Shock (as a rule)
- Swelling of the ankles

The two principal symptoms of an acute heart attack are pain (in the chest, upper abdomen, or shoulder and down the left arm) and extreme shortness of breath. The symptoms can occur together, but usually one or the other is stronger. Indigestion, nausea, and vomiting are often associated with a heart attack.

First Aid

To give first aid after a heart attack has occurred—
1. Place the victim in a comfortable position. Usually, sitting up is the best position, particularly if there is shortness of breath. However, the victim's comfort is a good guide. Use as many pillows as needed.
2. Provide ventilation and guard against drafts and cold.
3. If the victim is not breathing, begin artificial respiration.
4. Have someone call for an ambulance equipped with oxygen and have the victim's own doctor notified.
5. If the victim has been under medical care, help with the prescribed medicine.
6. Do not give liquids to an unconscious victim.

7. Since transportation throws added strain upon the victim, do not attempt to transport the victim until you get medical advice, if it is available within a reasonable time.

8. If you have been trained in cardiopulmonary resuscitation (CPR), and vital signs indicate CPR is needed, you should administer this resuscitation.

Stroke

A stroke (also called apoplexy) usually involves a spontaneous rupture of a blood vessel in the brain or formation of a clot that interferes with circulation.

Signs and Symptoms—Major Stroke

- Unconsciousness
- Paralysis or weakness on one side of the body
- Difficulty in breathing and in swallowing
- Loss of bladder and bowel control
- Unequal size of eye pupils
- Inability to talk or slurred speech

First Aid—Major Stroke

- Provide moderate covering.
- Maintain an open airway.
- Give artificial respiration if indicated.
- Position the victim so that secretions will drain from the side of the mouth.
- Call a doctor for medical advice as quickly as possible.
- *Do not* give fluids unless the victim is fully conscious and able to swallow and unless medical care will be delayed a long time.

Signs and Symptoms—Minor Stroke

In a minor stroke, small blood vessels in the brain are involved. These usually do not produce unconsciousness, and the symptoms depend upon the location of the hemorrhage and the amount of brain damage.

The minor stroke may occur during sleep and be accompanied by symptoms such as headache, confusion, slight dizziness, ringing in the ears, and other mild complaints. Later, there may be minor difficulties in speech, memory changes, weakness in an arm or leg, and some disturbance in the normal pattern of the personality.

First Aid—Minor Stroke

1. Protect the victim against accident or physical exertion.
2. Suggest medical attention.

Fainting

Description

Fainting is a partial or complete loss of consciousness due to a reduced supply of blood to the brain for a short time. Occasionally, a person collapses suddenly without warning. Recovery of consciousness almost always occurs when the victim falls or is placed in a reclining position, although injury may occur from the fall. To prevent a fainting attack, a person who feels weak and dizzy should lie down or bend over with the head at the level of the knees.

Fainting is usually preceded or accompanied by extreme paleness, sweating, coldness of the skin, dizziness, numbness and tingling of the hands and feet, nausea, and possible disturbance of vision.

First Aid

1. Keep victim lying down.
2. Loosen any tight clothing and keep crowds away.
3. If victim vomits, roll the person onto the side or turn the head to the side and, if necessary, wipe out the mouth with your fingers, preferably wrapped in cloth.
4. Maintain an open airway.
5. *Do not* pour water over victim's face because of the danger of aspiration; instead, bathe the face gently with cool water.
6. Do not give victim any liquid unless victim has revived.
7. Examine victim to determine whether or not the person has suffered injury from falling.
8. Unless recovery is prompt, seek medical assistance. Victim should be carefully observed afterward because fainting might be a brief episode in the development of a serious underlying illness.

Convulsions

A convulsion is an attack of unconsciousness, usually of violent onset. In an infant or small child, a convulsion may occur at the onset of an acute infectious disease, particularly during a period of high fever or severe gastrointestinal illness. Convulsions that develop later in the course of measles, mumps, and other childhood diseases are more serious and might reflect complications of the central nervous system.

Convulsions associated with head injury or brain disease, such as a tumor, an abcess, or a hemorrhage, often tend to be localized, with rigidity and jerking of groups of muscles instead of the whole body.

Signs and Symptoms

Convulsions are usually accompanied by—
* Rigidity of body muscles, usually lasting from a few seconds to perhaps half a minute, followed by jerking movements. (During the period of rigidity, victim may stop breathing, bite the tongue severely, and lose bladder and bowel control.)
* Bluish discoloration of face and lips
* Foaming at the mouth or drooling
* Gradual subsidence

First Aid

1. Prevent victim from hurting himself.
2. Give artificial respiration, if indicated.
3. *Do not* place a blunt object between victim's teeth.
4. *Do not* restrain victim.
5. *Do not* pour any liquid into victim's mouth.
6. *Do not* place a child in a tub of water.

If repeated convulsions occur, call for medical help immediately or take victim to a hospital.

Epilepsy

Description and Characteristics

Epilepsy is a chronic disease, usually of unknown cause, usually characterized by periodic convulsions ("grand mal seizures"). The victim may be able to lie down quickly, or the family may be able to tell that an attack is beginning by the sudden paleness of the victim's face or by the person's behavior. Mouth-to-nose resuscitation in providing artificial ventilation for victims of grand mal seizure is effective. Because of the high incidence of expiratory obstruction created by the soft palate, mouth-to-nose ventilation is the only effective way in which these victims can be ventilated. The mouth-to-nose technique must be accomplished in such a way that the mouth is left open for exhalation. If the teeth cannot be separated, the lips should be parted to permit passive exhalation. Much research has been carried out on epilepsy in recent years, and excellent preventive treatment is available; for this reason, physicians should determine the type and cause of every episode of convulsion.

A milder form of epilepsy occurs without convulsions. There may be only brief twitching of muscles, "petit mal" seizures, and momentary loss of contact with the surroundings. The victim may be seen staring fixedly at an object or off into the distance. This type of disturbance is less common than that which produces grand mal seizures.

First Aid

First aid for epilepsy is the same as for other convulsions, with primary effort being made to prevent the victim from hurting himself.

1. Push away nearby objects.
2. Do not force a blunt object between victim's teeth.
3. When jerking is over, loosen clothing around victim's neck.
4. Keep victim lying down.
5. Keep victim's airway open.
6. Prevent victim's breathing of vomit into the lungs by turning the head to one side or by having victim lie on the stomach.
7. If breathing stops, give artificial respiration.
8. After seizure, allow victim to sleep or rest. Provide privacy if possible.
9. If convulsions occur again, get medical help.
10. Do not allow a victim of convulsions to return to the water.

Prevention of Heart Attack and Apoplexy

The following measures may help to prevent a heart attack as well as apoplexy:

• Have a checkup every year after the age of 40.
• Control weight.
• Do not exercise strenuously if you are not used to exercise.
• Get adequate rest.

INDEX